THE HERESY OF DEMOCRACY

THE HERESY
OF DEMOCRACY

A Study in the History of Government

by

Lord Percy of Newcastle

HENRY REGNERY COMPANY
CHICAGO, ILLINOIS

Contents

I. The origin and pattern of democracy 1789–1939

MAY 6 1959

Acknowledgements

This study, I imagine, betrays its academic origin. In it I have drawn largely on some lectures of mine already published: the Riddell Memorial Lectures delivered in the University of Durham in 1944; the William Ainslie Memorial Lecture delivered at St Martin-in-the-Fields in 1945; and a lecture at the University of Natal in 1949. I acknowledge my indebtedness to these Foundations.

I am in much greater debt to the University of Oxford, whose teaching to my generation fifty years ago I have taken the liberty to criticize. I know, of course, that I owe this very liberty to it and that this gift is all that matters in University education. And to none do I owe more in this way than to Mr H. A. L. Fisher, whose name I have used to point a moral which he himself, I think, would have been the first to draw today.

Much of the ground over which I have wandered in the first part of this essay has now been more seriously covered by Mr J. L. Talmon in his *Origins of Total Democracy*. I have not found occasion to refer to his work, partly because I had already wandered far before it was published, but mainly because the essayist cannot travel with the scholar; he can only salute him at a distance.

The issue

An American friend, hearing that I contemplated this book, commented that to write "on the shortcomings of democracy is hitting a fellow when he's down, or shooting sitting ducks – particularly at this moment". Is this true? Is Democracy nowadays worth so long a commination service?

Certainly not, if it were only a question of the 'shortcomings' of a particular form of government. But the title of this book is seriously meant. It has been written in the conviction that, in the desperate insecurity of the modern world, what is at issue is not one more mistake in the technique of government, where every generation has multiplied its mistakes since the first syllable of recorded time, but a culminating error of belief which can be accurately described only in the language of religion. It is a false worship whose sincerest devotees, approaching their idol's shrine with the most unselfish aspirations, wake from their trance of adoration to find themselves bound unawares to the service of devils.

What is worse: the same bondage may await those who, with no real faith in the idol, repeat his litanies from habit, or because they have learnt no other creed. This has been – at least, as late as yesterday – the fashion of nine-tenths of the public men and active voters of the 'Free World', and even of their moral and spiritual guides. "There must be no propaganda in our schools", said a blameless English Professor of Education between the wars, "except, of course, propaganda for democracy...." "After all", wrote an equally blameless bishop to me during the General Strike in 1926, "we cannot deny the principle *vox populi vox Dei.*" Perhaps we, who have thus crowded the outer courts of the temple, are more on our guard today, for we have caught a glimpse of the real initiates of the inner shrine. G. K. Chesterton once said that satanism is "proud and sly, and always seems to be hiding a small mad smile"; and we can recognize now that unintended portrait of Nazidom and the Kremlin. But it is horrifying to think how we of the crowd thus paved these courts with our good intentions before 1939, and may still be paving them for a new hell soon to come.

For we have still, most of us, learnt no other creed. During all my youth and middle age, the language of belief was out of fashion in the world of parliamentary governments. The religion of all sensible men, which sensible men never tell, was enough for that world. Let a man subscribe to the social reform programme of his party and believe in what he pleased. We hardly yet realize how out of date this attitude has become today, when the whole policy of the Free World is concentrated in resistance to a false, but infectious, faith, built up perseveringly over a century and a half on the basis of the New Democracy of 1789. Or, if we have begun to realize it, we have unlearnt the only language in which our resistance to it can be expressed, not as a mere negation, but in terms of a positive counter-faith.

Does all this sound too rhetorical, too reminiscent of the style of a minor prophet? Perhaps; though, if I could master that style, I should be sorely tempted to write in it. At least it would fit my sense of urgency. But, anyway, that is not a style in which I could hope to convey my conviction of the nature of the issue. Another thing which the Free World has forgotten is how largely the language of belief is one of intellectual discrimination. We have failed to learn that lesson even from Lenin, and our failure accounts for the dangerous weakness of our resistance. Here again, the title of this book is seriously meant. Heresy is almost always very near to truth. Truth may stand on a rock, but it is seldom more than a narrow ledge; the gulf which separates it from error is bottomless, but a step can cross it. For instance, the distinction between a 'law-worthy' people (to borrow a primitive English phrase) and a sovereign people is a distinction of belief as to the nature of the authority which can be claimed by human government, but it is as narrow as it is deep – deep enough to make all the difference in practice between English-speaking and French parliamentary government, but narrow enough to seem mere hair-splitting to the modern Englishman, American or Frenchman.

Unfortunately, I am as little a logician as a prophet. Instead, I have chosen to write as a historian: to report distinctions, rather than to draw them; to trace causes and effects in the past, rather than to detect them in the present or predict them in the future. I do not pretend that my history is free from bias; but at least my bias is unconcealed. I have tried to understate, rather than overstate, my conclusions and my sense of the climax to which my story leads. Indeed, if I have failed to state any positive conclusion convincingly, I shall be content to have accustomed my readers to the use of a language in which they can state their own. One conclusion only I hope I have not understated: that the course of the world is determined by what men believe; and that the responsibility of belief is the greatest of the responsibilities which must be borne by a free people and by their governors.

I

The origin and pattern of democracy

The argument of these five chapters is that the Democratic State created by the French Revolution was a new creation, generically different from the older types of parliamentary 'democracy'. It has had a distinct philosophy from Rousseau to Marx and Lenin, a philosophy which is nothing less than a new religion. It has also a distinct constitutional pattern, from the Jacobin Club to Hitler and Stalin, a pattern in law-making, justice, political organization and the use of executive power. Its character is essentially totalist; failure to recognize this was the crucial mistake of the peace-makers in 1919; and this failure still cripples liberal statesmanship in the British Commonwealth and in the United States.

CHAPTER I

The birth of democracy

Peacemakers in 1919: the influence of nineteenth century fashions in history –
Newness of French revolutionary democracy in 1789 – Contrast with older
ideas of government by consent – Totalism and the blind spot of English
liberalism.

I

The members of the British 'governing class' who had to deal
with the problems of the new Europe after 1918 were, in
one way not well prepared for their task. It was a new class,
as newness is reckoned in England, and it was an academic, rather
than a social, class, for its typical element was the new Civil
Service, created by Mr Gladstone nearly fifty years before, on the
avowed principle that the British Empire could best be governed
by graduates of the Universities of Oxford and Cambridge.

For rather more than a generation, the experiment was amazing-
ly successful; but it was most successful, perhaps, while University
education remained severely classical. As University scholarship
turned to modern history and modern philosophy, University
teaching took, inevitably, the colour of current academic opinions
about government and social organization. Perhaps the best
representative of those opinions among University teachers at the
beginning of the twentieth century was Mr H. A. L. Fisher. To
him, later, writing the *History of Europe* between the two World
Wars, in days of comparative disillusionment, the historical era
inaugurated by the French Revolution was still the era of the
'Liberal Experiment'; if he had been writing thirty years earlier,
he would have best reflected current academic thought by calling
it the 'Liberal Achievement'.

To historians of this school, the French Revolution was not a catastrophe; it was hardly even a novelty; it merely opened the European chapter of an old story, whose earlier episodes had been the English Revolution of 1688 and the American Declaration of Independence. In 1919, the extreme example, almost the caricature, of this school was the American Woodrow Wilson. But for a typical leader of it we must turn to an earlier and much greater scholar. A quarter of a century before the Paris Conference, Lord Acton had opened his Cambridge lectures on the French Revolution with words which might have been almost appropriate to a description of the English Reform Bill crisis of 1832:

The revenue of France was near twenty millions when Louis XVI, finding it inadequate, called upon the nation for supply. In a single lifetime it rose to far more than one hundred millions, while the national income grew stilll more rapidly; and the increase was wrought by a class to whom the ancient monarchy denied its best rewards and whom it deprived of power in the country they enriched. As their industry effected change in the distribution of property and wealth ceased to be the prerogative of a few, the excluded majority perceived that their disabilities rested on no foundation of right and justice, and were unsupported by reasons of State. They proposed that the prizes in the Government, the Army and the Church should be given to merit among the active and necessary part of the people, and that no privilege injurious to them should be reserved for the unprofitable minority. Being nearly an hundred to one, they deemed that they were virtually the substance of the nation, and they claimed to govern themselves with a power proportioned to their numbers. They demanded that the State should be reformed, that the ruler should be their agent, not their master.

That is the French Revolution. To see that it is not a meteor from the unknown, but the product of historic influences which, by their union were efficient to destroy, and by their division powerless to construct, we must follow ... the procession of ideas that went before, and bind it to the law of continuity and the operation of constant forces.[1]

---

[1] Acton. *Lectures on the French Revolution,* Ch. 1. Macmillan 1910.

Lord Acton is too great a man for summary quotation. These words do not, in fact, fairly represent the lectures they introduce. It is the more remarkable that they do fairly reflect the peculiar reluctance of Victorian and Edwardian scholars to admit that anything really *happens* in history. History to them was continuity, development, progress, sometimes decay; but all so gradual that the event was merged in the process. To think of history in terms of catastrophe – to find room under the 'law of continuity' for phenomena as strange as the 'meteor' – savoured to them of a superstitious belief in 'Jewish apocalyptic'; indeed, this prejudice rather than any exact scholarship, determined the course of Biblical criticism in England and Germany for at least two generations.

In the particular case of European history since 1789, historians of this school were, above all, intent on dispelling that nightmare of 'The Revolution' as a new outburst of wickedness, which had haunted English Tories during the first half of the nineteenth century. Yet that nightmare was a reality, however unwise may have been the panic policies which it inspired. Something did happen in 1789 which had never happened before, and that something has determined the whole course of subsequent history. It happened on a late August day in 1789, when the States-General at Versailles voted, in their Declaration of the Rights of Man, the statement that

the principle of all sovereignty resides essentially in the nation; no body and no individual can exercise any authority which does not emanate expressly from the nation.

2

In making these words the foundation of the new constitution of France, the authors of the Declaration did not, of course, formulate a wholly new doctrine; but they created a new kind of State. The doctrine probably goes back to the very origins of human community life; it is certainly as old as Athens and Rome.

But, in the 1400 years since Europe first adopted the Christian faith as an official religion, it had never before been seriously asserted as a constitutional principle. For Christianity had introduced a new factor into political thought. It had formulated as revealed truth what had previously been no more than a tentative hope, except, to some extent, in the thought of an obscure people in Palestine: the belief in a personal law-giving God and in a divine purpose worked out by Him in human history. Since then, every political affirmation had involved a corresponding religious affirmation – or denial. The political idea of popular sovereignty had become inseparable from the religious idea of the 'inner light': that God's revelation of His law and purpose is conveyed solely and directly to each individual soul. From that affirmation Christendom had always shrunk as from a heresy. It was not only incompatible with the developed dogma of 'original sin', or with the hierarchical claims of the Church; it contradicted a much older instinct that man is naturally incapable, save under quite special guidance, of knowing God's law or serving His purpose. The admonition "Ye cannot serve the Lord, for He is a holy God" belongs to the most primitive record of the Hebrew settlement of Palestine.

Nineteenth-century scholars, writing under the influence of the French Revolution, were apt to distort the political ideas of the Middle Ages in this matter. A French scholar, for instance, thought that he could discern in Marsiglio of Padua's treatise *Defensor Pacis*

the essential three points of all democratic doctrine: that the legislative power belongs to the people: that the legislative power establishes the executive power; and that it judges, changes or deposes it if it fails in its duties.[1]

In fact, however, this is to misunderstand the whole mediaeval conception of Law. Only the first point represents mediaeval

---

[1] Janet, *Histoire de la Science Politique.*

thought, and that only in the sense that law was then regarded as the inherited possession of a people, to be maintained in its integrity and changed only very seldom, in case of absolute necessity, with the people's consent. In so far as the method of succession to executive power, by heredity or by election, was part of that law, the method could hardly be changed at all; and in so far as the acts of an executive might disregard the law, the people had an undefined right of resistance to it; but (if one may venture a sweeping generalization) it never occurred, even to the pamphleteers of the struggle between Papacy and Empire to regard the people as an active body of legislators or to argue that sovereign executive authority was itself derived from them. *Lex fit consensu populi et constitutione regis* was the modest maxim of French mediaeval jurists; and mediaeval thought about the much wider problem of the use of executive power was, perhaps, best represented by the formula of Nicholas de Cusa in the fifteenth century, which went no further than the assertion that a government's exercise of its authority "is to be accounted as divine when it proceeds from the general consent of its subjects".

After the Reformation, the Huguenot formula was very similar:

Princes are chosen by God, but are established by the people. . . . When a Prince is appointed, there is made between him and the people a covenant to the effect that obedience is to be rendered to him so long as he governs well.

That is a doctrine of a conditional divine right in the ruler and a conditional right, no less divine, in the citizen to rebel on just occasion. That formula passed from Europe to Puritan New England and thence, after being decently secularized to suit the taste of the eighteenth century, was written into the American Declaration of Independence. The formula of the drafters of that Declaration, only some fifteen years before the French Revolution, was that, in order to secure to all men their equal right to 'life, liberty and the pursuit of happiness', governments are instituted among men deriving their just powers from the consent of the governed.

That formula expresses, as well as any form of words can do, the distinctive nineteenth century conception, both of constitutional monarchy, as practised in England and sporadically imitated in other European countries, and of constitutional republicanism, as worked out in Switzerland and the United States.

The English-speaking world has drifted into the habit of giving this parliamentary form of government the name 'democracy', to the infinite confusion of clear thinking and the undermining of political integrity. Neither in theory nor in practice has it anything in common with the distinctive democracy of the French Revolution. In theory, it leaves undefined the ultimate source of political authority. Of course, to a Christian who knows what the powers of government are, it is unthinkable that any human being should claim to exercise them except by divine commission. But the explicit claim to such a commission has been so often made in an attempt to justify very questionable acts, that it has seemed to believers in parliamentary government better to treat this ultimate issue as a tacit assumption, and to concentrate attention rather on the purpose of governmental authority and on the limits within which it can be justly exercised. And, in practice, those who adopt this form of government do not pretend that its fundamental framework has been, or should be, instituted or agreed by the people. They commonly refuse, as did, for instance, the authors of the Union of South Africa, to submit a new constitution to a popular referendum. They are, indeed, frankly careless about origins. The fathers of the Constitution of the United States troubled themselves little about the authority for such purposes of the small group of gentlemen who drew it up, or of the State governments who accepted it. On the other hand, believers in parliamentary government are immensely careful that the acts of any political authority, however constituted, should be performed with the present consent of its citizens. The whole character of such government is determined by a belief in the lawful and unchallengeable transmission of authority in a State from generation to generation, and in a long and continuous process by which not only its law but the broad lines of its executive policy must be gradually worked out and adapted in accordance with popular wishes. When things go wrong, the process of law and policy, and even the transmission of authority, may have to be interrupted by some form of reformation or revolution; but such emergencies must not be allowed to obscure the normal character of settled government.

3

In contradiction to all this, the theory of the democratic State, as created in 1789, is solely the assertion of a dogma about the origin of political authority; its practise solely a demonstration that the dogma can be translated into action. The dogma is that, in any State, lawful authority to govern is the exclusive and inalienable possession of the whole body of citizens, by virtue of a consent which each is assumed to have given in the past; the demonstration is that an all-embracing citizen body can, in practice, be created which will, in fact, possess a united will to govern and be able to express and enforce that will.

Inevitably, this right to power comes to be regarded as over-riding all other rights, and questions of the purpose or limits of political authority tend, therefore, to occupy a very small place in democratic theory, and an even smaller one in democratic practice. As Mazzini[1] was to point out, half a century later, the Declaration of the Rights of Man of 1789, in so far as it asserted the 'natural and indefeasible rights' of the citizen against the State, marked the culmination of old eighteenth century 'analytical' ideas of individual liberty, while the introduction of demo-

---

[1] *Faith and the Future.* 1850.

cracy was to be distinguished by the 'synthetic' idea of *Association*. This is the germ of the modern communist formula in, for instance, China: "there is collective freedom, but no individual freedom". Of all the Rights declared in 1789, the only ones which survived the revolutionary process were the assertion of popular sovereignty and of the 'general will' as the basis of all law, and the twin assertion of equality as the indispensable means to the exercise of that sovereignty and to the formation and expression of that will. All democracy's eggs are always in the one basket; in other words, in the jargon of today, it is always 'totalitarian'.[1]

And, because all its eggs are in this one basket, it thrives on any political philosophy which, so to speak, enlarges and dignifies the basket. When, within a decade of Waterloo, Hegel propounded his idea of the Divine State as 'God walking on the earth', the State he intended to glorify was that of the Prussian monarchy and bureaucracy; but Marx saw that, for the construction of a philosophy of social democracy out of the fragments of Rousseau's 'social contract', it was necessary only to 'stand Hegel on his head'. For, in truth, the only kind of sovereign large enough to fill the giant frame of Hegel's Divine State is a sovereign people.

Of such is the political faith which has dominated European history since 1789. The initiative which it then won it has retained ever since. Its development from Jacobinism, through Bonapartism, Nationalism and Socialism, to the Totalist State of the twentieth century has been direct and unbroken, and has been determined throughout by a single theory of political authority. In all its forms it has had always the same character. Against it, throughout the supposed era of the 'Liberal Experiment', liberalism of the English-speaking type has been always on the defensive. Liberalism has constantly patronized it, or tried to make terms

---

[1] Jargon for jargon, 'totalist' is surely better and will be used in what follows.

with it, and has been as constantly disappointed. Thus Mr H. A. L. Fisher, as late as 1936, could write of

the great democratic maxim that the State should aim at securing the greatest happiness of the greatest number,

and of the conflict between Hegel's:

mystical conception of the State as divinity, and those theories deriving from Rousseau which regard it as a social contract based on voluntary choice and consent.[1]

So Rousseau, Mazzini and Marx become humble disciples of Bentham; Marx's debt to Hegel is forgotten; and the assumed creative act of a sovereign people in constituting a supreme government is confounded with the actual consent of an electorate to the particular acts of a parliament. Liberalism may know its enemy, but it is often fatally mistaken in its allies.

One day, the history of the 150 years from 1789 to 1939 will be written from this point of view, in the language of high tragedy. That task is beyond the scope of this essay; all that can be attempted here is to sketch some of the constant characteristics of pure democracy, as revealed in action during this century and a half, and to suggest the true issue between it and its only possible alternative in the modern world.

---

[1] *History of Europe,* Ch. xxxvi.

CHAPTER 2

Democracy as religion : Rousseau, Mazzini and Fichte

How to generate a 'General Will' – The 'inner light' and 'sentiments of sociability' – Incompatibility of democracy and Christianity – Equality, Christian and totalist – Enthusiasm and 'spontaneity' – The 'Nation made Man' by State education.

I

The first and fundamental characteristic of democracy is that it is an exclusive religion.

Of that religion Rousseau was the first prophet. He not only gave a new twist to the old political philosophy of the 'social contract'; he also founded that philosophy, explicitly and inseparably, on a new formulation of the religious doctrine of the 'inner light'. Any State, he asserted, existed solely by virtue of an act of association assumed to have been executed by all its citizens. Sovereignty in the State was, therefore, vested by right in the whole body of the citizens, who were enabled to exercise it directly at all times by an instinctive knowledge of natural law implanted by a Supreme Being in the mind of every man and expressing itself inevitably in the 'general will' of all citizens. "Has he not" said Rousseau's Savoyard Vicar,

has he not bestowed on me conscience to love the good, reason to ascertain it, freedom to choose it?

Thus far, the new religion sounds like a mere echo of eighteenth century deism, or an anticipation of the milder forms of nineteenth century rationalism. Its obvious challenge to all forms of theocratic authority was to commend it, as time went on, alike to English non-conformists and to continental anti-clericals; it was,

26

indeed, the chief of those family likenesses that misled English liberals into their attempted alliances with democracy. Long afterwards Acton, the Liberal Catholic, remarked, with some naïveté, on the odd drafting of Article 10 of the Rights of Man:

None shall be molested for his opinions, even his religious opinions.

"It would appear", he said,

that toleration was that part of the liberal dogma for which the deputies (of the States General) were least prepared.[1]

But of course. The deputies were not engaged in freeing men to think as they pleased; they were constructing a power plant to be driven by men who should all think alike. How could toleration be allowed to intrude its alien elements into the crucial alchemy which was to fuse the people into one, and mould in them a single General Will?

For Rousseau's gospel of personal illumination did not stop at his Savoyard Vicar. Since faith in that gospel was the only fundamental law, it must, he went on to argue, be specially promulgated and enforced by the State. Belief in

the existence of a divinity, powerful, intelligent, benevolent and providential; in the life to come, the happiness of the righteous, the punishment of the wicked; in the sanctity of the social contract and of the laws,

must be made compulsory on all citizens, not as religious dogmas, but as *Sentiments of Sociability* without which the people's great Act of Association would be insecure. And it was in that spirit that the Declaration of August 1789 was stated by its authors to be made 'in the presence of the Supreme Being'.

Since this Being is not much more than a personification of the democratic State, he can personify Marx's determinism – or, indeed, Hegel's Divine State – as easily as Rousseau's law of

---

[1] *Op. cit.*, Ch. vii.

nature. Perhaps his most appropriate incarnation is Mazzini's Nationality:

Every people has a special mission which co-operates towards the general work achieved by Humanity. That mission, determined by its ethnographic, territorial and historical conditions, constitutes its Nationality; and Nationality is sacred.

But one thing this Supreme Being cannot be; he cannot be the Christian God. For a compulsory Sentiment of Sociability must expressly exclude any religion which teaches a divided loyalty or a dual standard of conduct. To Marx and Rousseau alike the belief, fundamental to Christianity from its earliest days, in a citizenship of heaven transcending the citizenships of earth, must be the most unsocial of all possible sentiments. "Anything", said Rousseau,

Anything that breaks social unity is worthless; all institutions which set a man in conflict with himself are worthless;

even a quietest Christianity is 'contrary to the social spirit', for

so far from attaching the hearts of the citizens to the State, it detaches them from it, as from all earthly things.

Mazzini translated this language, very nebulously, into terms of historical development. His gospel was

one single God; one single master, the law of God; one single inter-preter of the law, Humanity,

and he must, therefore, he said,

reject all doctrine of external revelation, of any immediate or final character, and substitute for it the slow, continuous and indefinite revelation of the designs of Providence through the collective Life of Humanity.

For practical purposes, of course, the 'collective life of humanity' means the State. The logic of the democratic argument could not, in 1789 or in 1848, and cannot now, tolerate any Church which is more, or other, than a domestic chaplain to the State.

This is the real issue which, to the surprise and confusion of moderate men of both parties, has produced the irrepressible conflict between pure democracy and the Christian faith. From the outset, the real nature of this conflict was blurred by the tragic twist in Christian doctrine which had substituted for the dualism between an earthly and a heavenly citizenship the rivalry between two centres of earthly allegiance, secular and ecclesiastic. It has been against that distortion of Christian truth, embodied alike in the Gallican Church of eighteenth-century France and in the ultramontane Church of Rome of the mid-nineteenth century, that the democratic movement has been, above all, a revolt. In the earlier phases of each stage in that revolt, it has been easy for the rebels to appear, even to themselves, as no more than anti-clericals. The drafters of the Civil Constitution of the Clergy in 1790, for example, thought they could prohibit all legal recognition of Papal authority without destroying

the unity of faith and communion with the visible Head of the Universal Church.

Later, the democrats of Italy could honestly take refuge in the formula which Cavour had stolen from French liberal Catholics, and spoilt in stealing: 'a free Church in a free State'. But the real underlying issue remained, to be made clear at last by the dictatorships of the twentieth century at Moscow and Berlin.

We shall have to return later to the history of the relations of the democratic State and the Christian Church. Here it is sufficient to note the issue on which these relations have always turned and to add some further notes on the religion of democracy.

2

Religion always asserts the Equality of all men. In a sense, that is what religion is for. But obviously, no two human beings can be equated in their totality. To assert their equality is to make a judgment of value, to believe that certain characteristics common to both have a special importance to each. To make such a judgement is an essential function of religion. Primitive or debased religion asserts the equal liability of all men to the arbitrary action of the gods, or their equal dependence upon the processes of nature. From that, at ascending levels, religions have asserted the equal subjection of all men to a divine moral law, or their equal son-ship to the fatherhood of a single or a supreme God. At the Christian level, the assertion has been expressed in a more compelling language, which has been the origin of all that seems to most of us most lovely in the social life of the Western Continents, and most enduring in their law. As thus:

Albeit God hath ordained distinction and difference in the regiment and administration of civil policies, yet in the hope of the life to come He hath made all equal. Of the prince doth God require that he refuse himself and that he follow Christ Jesus; of the subject He requireth the same. Neither is any of God's children so poor but that he hath thus much to bestow upon the ornaments and maintenance of their spiritual tabernacle; neither yet is there any so rich of whose hands God requireth any more.[1]

But it is also possible for the lawgiver, not thus to ascertain and register men's essential equalities, but, in despair at their intractable inequalities, to give them an equality of his own for his own purposes, as equal subjects of a king, or equal voters in a republic, or equal members of a nation. Up to a point, the argument for such a levelling policy is overwhelmingly strong; distinctions between citizens, carried beyond fairly narrow limits, are incompatible wiih the business efficiency of governments. But 'equality before the law', based on these grounds alone, is a spiritless thing. Its two chief agents are the tax-gatherer and the technologist: the one seeking to reduce men to manageable units of assessment for the collection of revenue, the other to manage-

---

[1] John Knox. *Letter to the Commonalty of Scotland* – 1558.

able units of labour for handling the instruments of production. Thence, it is easy, as the business of the State grows, to extend the field of levelling to reduce all children, for instance, to manageable units for the purposes of a comprehensive system of State school-ing. Equality of this kind for 'reasons of State' seems to be the almost necessary condition of all State action; and that, to many minds, is the main objection to the indefinite extension of the field of State action which is the characteristic of all modern 'progressive' governments.

But democracy makes a virtue of this necessity. In its philosophy, the 'reason of State' becomes a religion of the State. The equality of all men is a necessary assumption if all men are to be assimilated into one citizen body and their wills into a single General Will. It is a 'sentiment of sociability' more fundamental even than belief in a Supreme Being. And if the facts contradict the assumption, they must be changed. The unassimilable must be eliminated; eccentricities and superiorities are alike 'anti-social'; indeed, every form of life is anti-social which is differentiated in any way from the mass of life of common citizenship. All such life is 'privilege', and as such it must be rooted out. The latest example of this argument today (1953) is the proposal of the English Labour Party to abolish, first, all Grammar Schools and, eventually, all independent schools.

This is, indeed, democracy's characteristic Mark of the Beast. As we shall see, of all the means of assimilation, the most essential to democracy is a uniform State-controlled education.

3

Religion can bring men to a unity of belief by two methods: by rational exposition, coupled with the sobrieties of formal worship, and by emotional 'prophecy' directed to provoke enthusiasm. But the deism of Rousseau and Mazzini was beyond all rational argument, and a sense of humour has deterred later democrats from trying to reproduce the ritual which Robespierre invented for the worship of the Supreme Being.[1] The religion of democracy must, therefore tend to live, not by reason, but by enthusiasm.

A people claiming to be sovereign must not only, in the words of Edmund Burke, "form itself into a mass which has a true political personality", it must assert that it is already such a mass. From the outset, it must demonstrate that it is united enough to govern. Under all other theories of politics, national unity is the product of a national habit of government; under the theory of popular sovereignty, national unity must itself create that habit. A people must rush into unity or remain in anarchy. This contrast between the slowly ripening fruit of old experience and what Danton called

the bronze seething and foaming and purifying itself in the cauldron

was the whole burden of Burke's famous indictment of the Revolution.

The strength of that indictment does not lie merely in the fact that a hectic search for unity must entail mob violence and legalized terror; it lies in the more fundamental fact that a people, thus summoned to demonstrate its unity as the pre-condition of its liberty, must regard enthusiasm as the first duty of citizenship. The efficient action of the cauldron depends wholly upon its temperature. We miss the point if we laugh off, as mere posturing, the rhetoric of revolutionary orators or the jargon of revolutionary mob leaders. All this was the deliberate and necessary blast of the furnace. In that context, Robespierre's programme of 'terror sustaining virtue' was perfectly logical. In a hundred reports to the French Convention in the later months of 1792, the first months of the 'Republic, One and Indivisible', the 'people' meant, quite

---

[1] The exception to this generalisation is Comte's attempt, towards the end of his life, to provide 'positivism' with a catechism and a ritual. But the fate of that attempt is an additional illustration of our point.

soberly and by definition, any active body of individuals in a rage, in contrast to all quiescent, and therefore presumably lukewarm, citizens.

The passion which unites the oppressed against their oppressors is as old as history; but the transfiguration of this natural passion of vengeance into a creative political virtue, to be carefully inculcated and fostered, was the most characteristic feature of the French Revolution and has been, perhaps, its most lasting effect. It came to be a sufficient justification of any system of government that, in Louis Blanc's phrase about the Paris Commune of 1792, 'it breathes heroism'. In the heated atmosphere of democratic propaganda, as Guizot wrote in his memoirs, "insult becomes a routine and fury a habit". Sixty years after the first revolution, de Tocqueville, watching the Paris mob invading the National Assembly of 1848, remarked that they seemed to be play-acting, without serious intent, a fury which they had been taught to regard as revolutionary good form. A quarter of a century later still, Marx noted the 'spontaneity' of the Paris Commune of 1871 as its most admirable feature, and that word, with all its implications, came to occupy, in the communist creed, as developed by Lenin, the same sort of doctrinal place as is occupied in Christian theology by the word 'grace'. Thus 'spontaneity' became in 1918 the title of the Soldiers' and Workers' Soviets to be regarded as the basis of the Russian Socialist State, in preference to any artificial system of government which might emerge from a constituent convention.

The culmination of the story may be conveniently marked by the Russian general election on the occasion of the new constitution of 1936, which has been thus described by a friendly English observer:

This people has a genius for a cosmic emotion, which makes of them a mystical unity; and they responded to the call with a self-abandonment in which there was something dionysiac. To have felt and realised,

c

though for a moment, this generous excitement, and to have given expression to it in the quasi-sacrament of the nearly unanimous vote, was a contribution to political education.[1]

Such is the democratic idea of political education; such is the tradition of enthusiasm which has re-appeared in every European movement of nationalism, from Mazzini's Young Italy of 1831 to the Fascist and Hitler youth of the 1930s. Its language has been caught up even by sober and sceptical Liberal scholars like Renan, who could define a 'nation' as a union formed by any group of people 'in the heat of their heart'. The growing intensity of enthusiasm required by current democratic doctrine is indicated by the replacement of one enthusiastic title for the common man by another, of the 'citizen' of the first revolution by the 'comrade' of modern socialism. Democracy has, indeed, raised acutely the question how, if at all, the sentiment of brotherhood can be made safe for mankind. Today, the highest praise that can be given to any political movement is to draw attention to its 'democratic fervour', and we are, to our cost, only too familiar, in the conduct of contemporary international relations, with the 'routine of insult and habit of fury' which appears to be inseparable from such fervour.

4

This growing intensity has, however, been most significantly marked by a development in the means of producing it. It is not only that the technical equipment of propaganda has changed. The elaboration of this technique can be traced, amusingly enough, through the bulletins of Napoleon I and the banquet speeches of Napoleon III to the broadcasting of Goebbels and the Kremlin. But, much more dangerously, the technique has changed by the enlistment of the processes of public education in the task of unifying and activating the 'General Will' of the sovereign

---

[1] Maynard. *The Russian Peasant and other Studies.* 1942.

people. To this end the democratic State must make very sure that it exercises a monopoly of education and that this monopoly is consciously directed to produce, not only the right kind of citizen with the right kind of will and opinion, but a sufficient number of the same kind of citizens with the same kind of will and opinion.

Of course, all despots wish to monopolize education and, to that end, all have wished to turn the Christian Church into a domestic chaplain to the State. As Voltaire wrote to Catherine the Great's minister in 1768:

It is only your illustrious sovereign who knows how to reign; she pays the priests; she opens or closes their mouth at her pleasure.

But no one can mistake the special tang of doctrinal bitterness which characterizes the democratic monopoly. It has set the problem of Church schools in the very forefront of French politics for 150 years, from the establishment of the Napoleonic *Université Impériale* in 1807 down to the wreckage of a whole series of Cabinets in the successive crises of 1951. Its typical exponent was the Gambetta of 1871:

In place of the clerical doctrine . . . which insists that man is a plaything in God's hand, the Revolution teaches that right reason is sovereign, that the will of man is decisive and responsible. . . . For eighty years these two systems have stood face to face. . . . They have waged in the very heart of society an internecine conflict whence results that lack of system in our education which has robbed society of its equilibrium. . . . Leave to the Churches the religious world. . . . Ours is a modern world which thirsts after knowledge, truth, freedom, equality, which seeks to declare and discharge social duties by exalting and emancipating the humanity common to high and low alike.[1]

In educational policy, this doctrine has set the example which tends today to be unthinkingly copied by countries whose creed is

---

[1] Quoted from Stannard, *Gambetta*. Methuen, 1921.

liberty: the example which in France is called the *école unique;* in Germany the *Einheitsschule,* and now in England the *comprehensive school.* It was reserved for Hitler to give it its right name: the name of *Gleichschaltung.*

Indeed, this philosophy of an education directed to the moulding of the General Will of a sovereign people is historically a peculiar German contribution to democratic doctrine, uncomplicated by the special issue of anti-clericalism which has dominated French thought. One German in particular may be taken as the prophet of this philosophy. The ex-Jacobin Fichte launched in 1810, in his *Addresses to the German Nation,* what was, in effect, a new mysticism of nationalist education. To him the Nation was the incarnation of all human hopes of immortality; patriotism must, therefore, be conceived, not as

the spirit of a calm love of the constitution and the laws, but (as) the devouring flame of that higher love of one's native country which sees the Nation as the garment of the Eternal.

To kindle that flame was the sole function of the State:

The State is but the means to the higher end of an eternal education: the progressive and symmetrical development of pure manhood in the Nation.

That is *Gleichschaltung* a century before the word was coined. And Fichte clinched his gospel in a phrase much more startling, which to a Christian has all the implications of blasphemy:

Progress is that perfection of education by which the Nation is made Man.

Such is the language of democratic enthusiasm. After more than a century, we are at last learning that such rhapsodies, however absurd they may sound to an English ear, must be taken seriously. And we may be the more ready to take seriously also the counter-rhetoric, at first sight no less inflated, of continental conservatives. Chateaubriand, for instance, may have been not far wrong, a few years after 1810, in prophesying the doom of Christian civilization:

The days of the desert have come back. Christianity will have to begin afresh in the sterility of the Thebaid, surrounded by a world of idolatry: man's terrible idolatry of himself.

CHAPTER 3

Democracy as religion: Socialism and social-ism

Marx's solution of the problem of the General Will – Marxian eschatology: the classless society and the abolition of the Immoral State – Non-Marxian social-ism in the west: the degeneration of political into social philosophy; planning as a substitute for law.

I

All the same, throughout the nineteenth century it was not the old faith but the new idolatry that seemed repeatedly condemned to start afresh in the desert. After 1815, it had to retire there until, as Napoleon at St Helena foresaw, it had learned to adapt itself to the new movement of nationalism, which it had inspired but never understood. Then, when it had clothed itself in its new garb, the fruits of its brief revivalist successes in 1848 were gathered, during the next twenty-five years, by apparently more sober types of nationalism, monarchist or republican. From the desert, it continued to leaven political thought, but it never became the cement of a democratic State. In the desert it would have remained, if Marx had not added to it the new element that precipitated its prophetic ecstasies into a coherent creed.

This is the real significance of the dogma of economic determinism. The mere transition of democracy from the uncertain individualism of 1789 to the nascent socialism of 1848 is of minor importance; the fundamental principles of 1789 were bound to be applied to property as soon as, in the new economy of the industrial revolution, the development of trade and industry and the distribution of its proceeds became major objects of State policy.[1]

From its beginnings, democratic doctrine had suffered from two allied weaknesses. One was the difficulty of devising any normal and rational method of generating the unity of thought and purpose postulated by the theory of the General Will, or of enabling it to express itself when generated. The other was the shadowy character of the semi-religious sanctions to which that Will is supposed to conform. Unity could apparently be produced only by successive gusts of enthusiasm. Rousseau's sentiments of sociability were, after all, merely sentiments, and Mazzini's God was, as Chesterton said of the Kaiser's, "neither a master nor a servant, but only a convenient synonym." It had been the same with the dogma of 'human perfectibility', which had commended itself especially to English philosophic Radicals; it had proved impossible to construct any coherent idea either of the causes of human imperfection or of the way to their removal, for only a German could believe in Fichte's dream of regeneration by a system of State education.[2]

---

[1] 'When the right to property was no more than the origin and foundation of many other rights, it could be defended without difficulty, or, rather, it was not attacked. But today when the right to property appears to be only the last remnant of an aristocratic world which has been destroyed, an isolated privilege in the midst of a levelled society . . . it has to stand alone in resisting the direct and incessant assault of democratic opinion'. De Tocqueville. October, 1847.

[2] In this remark the emphasis is, of course, on the words 'regeneration' and 'State'. Many men who pitch their social ideals lower than the religious level have put an exaggerated confidence in mere education. The 'diffusion of knowledge' was the characteristic catchword of continental freemasonry throughout the eighteenth century. Later, in England, James Mill, his son recorded, "felt that all would be gained if the whole population were taught to read, if all sorts of opinion were allowed to be addressed to them by word and in writing, and if, by means of the suffrage, they could nominate a legislature to give effect to the opinions they adopted". Such hopes are still common, especially in the teaching profession; but they belong to the attitude which we are about to describe as 'social-ism', not to the dogmatic creed of pure democracy.

But the developed theory of economic determinism has changed the whole character of the argument. From the clouds of twisted philosophy and history in which that theory is wrapped emerges one simple, and eminently expoundable, proposition: that men who gain their livelihood by working together in the same occupation will inevitably think alike, provided that all motives for competitive self-seeking can be eliminated from their co-operation. At root there can be only one such anti-social motive: the desire for individual ownership of the means of production, or individual control over the distribution of the product; and this motive can be eradicated by the determined establishment of collective ownership and control. Collectivization thus becomes the only function of the new society involving the exercise of *political power;* all else will be mere *administration* of the processes of communal production and sale, the management of *things,* not persons, requiring no *State* machinery for its conduct. Eventually, therefore, the State will 'wither' away, to be superseded by the quiet *socialism* of classless and communally minded economic groups.

From this drastic philosophical simplification of the problems of government several conclusions follow. The first problem of all democracy is to define 'the people' who are to be the sovereign body. Sooner or later, this always means some sort of purge of anti-social or non-national elements. But the Marxist definition is simpler and more rational. The people, henceforward, are only and solely the workers, the 'proletariat'. For them, instinctive enthusiasm is superseded, as the motive power of the General Will, by an apparently scientific psychology. More, at the crucial formative stage of the revolutionary process, the General Will itself is superseded by a sort of fundamental law. At that stage, democratic government, rechristened 'the dictatorship of the proletariat', is liberated even from such residual constitutional restraints as had hampered, in theory if not in practice, earlier experiments in revolutionary method. The executives of that dictatorship have only one task: to purge society of all non-proletarian elements. In that task they have no need, and in truth no right, to consult the wishes of the sovereign people, for *ex-hypothesi*, till the purge is completed, a true people does not exist and the people's will is radically corrupt. A revolutionary government must, therefore, have an independent discretion in establishing collectivization as absolute as that of the Supreme Court of the United States in interpreting a written constitution. Indeed, since the General Will can come into real existence only in a Utopia where it will no longer have any *political* work to do, it will never be necessary to devise any machinery for its political expression. When that Utopia is reached, the dubious exercise of political powers will no longer have any place in the 'spontaneous cohesion of virtuous wills' which, forty years ago, a Conservative writer portrayed as the ultimate end of political liberty, to be realized only in the Christian's ideal City of God.[1]

2

This quotation from the opposite pole of belief is strictly in point. Many critics have observed that Marxism, in spite of its professed hatred of religion, is itself a religion; but perhaps few have realized how genuine a religion it is. Like all vital religions, its focus is, not merely in a faith, but in a hope. Socialism, through which alone the General Will of the sovereign people can express itself, is a future condition of blessedness, at least as remote in time and as indefinable in character as the New Jerusalem; and Marxists, like some early Fathers of the Christian Church, have had to fight their hottest battles against Utopian heretics, from Proudhon to Herbert Morrison, who have aspired to anticipate the promise of that blessedness by experiments in communal co-operation under the conditions of an unregenerated world. The Russian revolutionaries were to discover the practical wisdom

---

[1] Lord Hugh Cecil. *Liberty and Authority*. 1910.

of Marx's teaching on this point when they found how incompatible was the old Russian peasant commune with the dictatorship of the proletariat. In much the same way, the Christian reformers of the sixteenth century had found that anabaptist attempts to anticipate 'the glorious liberty of the children of God' were incompatible with the existence of any organized Church.

Yet, at the same time, as in all vital religions, this hope of the future, unrealizable in the present, is nevertheless so organically linked with things as they are as to afford a guide to present duty and an incentive to present action. For example, the unanimity of the ideal classless society, unattainable now, can and must be reflected now in the 'spontaneity' of revolutionary action. As in Christian teaching, the promised salvation transcends all possible present virtue, not by contradicting, but by fulfilling it.

Indeed, the analogy with Christian teaching is closer even than this. Much of the political language of Russian Communism is comprehensible only if it is accepted as the genuine language of religion. In terms of Western political thought, the citizen of a totalist State cannot be 'free', either in the Russia of today or in the Roman Empire of the first century; but the Russian who believes that he has, even now, been emancipated from the mental and moral corruption of capitalism, may claim a more real freedom than any immunity from political restraints, just as genuinely as the Christian of the first century could claim to have been 'made free from sin'.[1]

This development in the religion of democracy is accompanied, as one would expect, by a change in its language, from the rhetoric of moral exhortation and condemnation, in which even the Communist Manifesto of 1848 was mainly written, to the technical terms of dogmatic definition. To some extent, this was Lenin's special work in his long controversy with the Mensheviks before 1914. All social democracy's eggs are still in the one

---

[1] See the second footnote on p. 51 for an instance of this sort of claim.

basket, but the basket now is a theory, not so much of the source of political power, as of the inexorable condition of human salvation. Its enemy is therefore, not so much any political 'petty-bourgeois reaction', as heretical 'deviation' from the true gospel among its own adherents. It still relies on enthusiasm, but enthusiasm must be more strictly canalized within the framework of dogma. Its censorship of opinion, must be intensified, for the slightest distraction of men's attention away from disinterested economic co-operation, as the one means to human regeneration, or the slightest doubt cast on the effectiveness of that co-operation, will destroy all rational hope for mankind. Science can be tolerated only in so far as it increases and stimulates confidence in man's power over nature; the Church can no longer play even the part of domestic chaplain to the State; at best it can become one of the means of a necessary physiological relaxation for tired workers, on the same plane as the picture gallery or the ballet.[1]

Unfortunately for this imposing dogmatic edifice, the future hope of communal blessedness cannot reflect itself in one essential sphere of present life: in the *present political action of the State*. These two are not *in pari materia* at all. There is, in the Communist's canon, no Old Testament on which he can fall back, as, even in its dreariest moments, the Christian Church has been able to fall back, to find some moral purpose for a State unable to measure itself by higher standards. This may yet prove to be the fatal disease of communism, for, as we have suggested, it is becoming increasingly difficult, even for the faithful, genuinely to believe in the prospect of getting rid of State law. Already in Lenin's later writings, the 'withering' of the State had begun to recede into the distance. And, as it fades, the gap between present imperfection and future blessedness can be filled only by an

---

[1] Naturally, it has also, in the international situation of today, a special usefulness as a means of propaganda in Christian countries; but, in the ideology of social democracy, this is, of course, a transitory function.

essentially arbitrary political power. It has become flagrantly manifest in communist societies that the protection of communal property against 'sabotage' is as necessary an object of State law as is, in other societies, the protection of private property against fraud or damage, but with this difference: that the change tends to enlarge the sphere of criminal, and reduce that of civil, law. And, obviously, the punishment of a criminal can be arbitrary in a way that an adjudication between two private litigants cannot be.[1] Much more, therefore, than in other vital religions, the decay of eschatological hope leaves the communist citizen at the mercy of arbitrary governments whom, by reason of his still corrupt nature, he must confess himself radically unfit to judge or control. Dostoievsky's Grand Inquisitor, for whom the aim of wise government is to minister to the material well-being of citizens unfit to be free, and particularly unfit to receive the full truths of religion, may have been a salutary satire on the tendencies of the worst Christian rulers; but it is an exact portrait of the best possible rulers who have been trained in the school of Marx and Lenin.[2]

3

If these have been the effects of socialist doctrine on the belief and practice of revolutionary democrats, its effects on other schools of political thought have been just as remarkable. It has powerfully stimulated its disciples, but it has no less powerfully drugged its opponents. Its conception of politics and the State

---

[1] Thus in 1938 the maximum penalty for 'counter-revolutionary' crimes was extended to 25 years imprisonment, as against the ten-year maximum of the Penal Code.

[2] English socialist scholars, like the late H. J. Laski, have argued that these results flow from a Leninist corruption of the quite liberal and broad-minded principles of Marx and Engels. It may be so. Our argument here is that they both flow from an older source; the principle of democracy in all its dogmatic forms. This, of course, was Marx's and Engels' own view, for they insisted that bourgeois democracy must precede the social revolution.

as inherently vicious and illiberal has threatened to discredit all political thinking, and to divert almost the whole modern educated world from the study of the State into the study of some vaguer entity called 'society'.

This might fairly be called the Romantic Movement of the late nineteenth and early twentieth centuries. It had affinities with the Romantic Movement in literature a century earlier. In it Education often took the place occupied in the earlier period by Imagination. Such 'social', as distinct from political, study has some real meaning for the socialist who accepts the Marxist doctrine that the sole origin and purpose of State law has been the protection of private property, and that a social union, transcending such law, will result automatically from the collectivization of property. But to those who do not hold this doctrine, the renunciation of political, in favour of 'social', thought is meaningless. It amounts to leaving State law to look after itself, without any prospect of ever being able to get rid of it. And what we have said about the threatened bankruptcy of a communism which loses its eschatological hopes, is surely at least a warning of the danger of discarding political philosophy and the principles of civilized law, in order the better to concentrate on the study of social welfare and the formation of what, in the jargon of the day, is called a 'social conscience'. It is a warning against that habit of mind which judges acts according to whether they are, not lawful or unlawful, just or unjust, or even right or wrong, but 'social' or 'anti-social'.

Yet this kind of misty and hyphenated 'social-ism' is what the schools and universities of almost the whole Western world are now increasingly thinking and teaching – let alone less highly educated centres of thought. In the United States, the existence of a written constitution, and the dominant position of Law Schools and of the legal profession, tends to keep the evil within bounds, but, even so, much of the fashionable attempt, in America as well as in Britain, to 'educate for citizenship' takes this social-ist form. Next to the 'social conscience', the pet social-ist phrase is 'economic democracy'. This phrase does not mean that, in the words of 1789, 'no body and no individual can exercise any authority' in any economic enterprise, 'which does not emanate expressly from the nation'; it does not imply that economic activity should not continue to be based on private property; it implies only that, as a matter of legal rights, such property should be perpetually insecure. In this academic flight from the State, political and even economic history must give place to 'social' history, law to 'sociology', political science to anthropology; while the crucial issue of civic obedience disintegrates into 'allegiance to environment' – as who might say 'the old school tie'.

All this has a nightmare resemblance, in the recent past, to the Russian decree of February 1918 which directed the courts to interpret existing law in the light of the 'revolutionary conscience'. Even more, in the remote past, it is fantastically reminiscent of the degenerate Roman cult of *Fortuna*, the Luck of the State, or of *Romanitas*, the pattern of behaviour proper to Roman citizenship. Alike to Socrates and to Hampden, at an interval of two thousand years, the whole social inheritance of Athens or England was solidified into a *Lex Terrae*, the Laws of the City or the Law of the Land. But the modern social-ist, like the citizen of imperial Rome, dissolves even positive law back into the gases of sentiment and tradition. He speaks, for instance, of the British or the American 'way of life'; he has never heard of *Romanitas*, and he does not realize how near he is to *Deutschtum*.

How near may, perhaps, be measured by one quotation. In 1906, the father of this school of thought in America, Lester Ward, concluded a quarter of a century of writing by the publication of his *Applied Sociology*. At the end of this book, he developed as follows the idea of 'attractive legislation', which should replace 'mandatory and prohibitory laws'.

It must not be supposed that such legislation can be conducted to any considerable extent in the open sessions of legislative bodies. These will doubtless need to be maintained, and every new law should be finally adopted by a vote of such bodies, but more and more this will become a merely formal way of putting the final sanction of society on decisions that have been carefully worked out in what may be called the sociological laboratory. Legislation will consist in a series of exhaustive experiments on the part of true scientific sociologists and sociological inventors, working on the problems of social physics from the practical point of view. It will undertake to solve not only questions of general interest to the State – the maintenance of revenue without compulsion and without friction, and the smooth and peaceful conduct of the operations of a nation, – but questions of social improvement, the amelioration of the condition of all people, the removal of whatever privations may still remain, and the adoption of means to the positive increase of the social welfare, in short of the organization of human happiness.[1]

It is by no mere chance that the extraordinary naïveté of this picture reminds us in 1953 so forcibly of some of the main features of Nazi Germany: of a rubber-stamp legislature registering dictatorial decrees; of a State Church, devoted to 'positive Christianity'; and of S.S. laboratories working out, in the gas-chamber and under the hypodermic syringe, the 'scientific' means to social improvement. For if, as in Lester Ward's philosophy, ethics means only the 'socialization of knowledge', and if 'all real knowledge is science', the rights of individual human beings must always be insecure, however impressively this or that sociologist may assert his personal belief in the equal rights of all members of society.

In Britain this social-ism has come increasingly to determine the whole policy of governments. Englishmen are supposed to have a special right to play with fire and a natural immunity to its effects; but let us at least recognize what we are doing. We can

---

[1] *Applied Sociology*. Ginn & Co. pp. 338–9.

now see how right is the Marxist who contrasts the social administration of things with the political government of persons. He
is wrong only in preferring administration to statesmanship.
Nowadays we are all preoccupied with urgent administrative
projects to deal with the problems of 'social physics': with housing
or school-building campaigns to overtake a shortage, with business agreements between miners and the Coal Board to increase
production, with periodical patchings of old age pensions or
unemployment benefits, with rate relief to industry and agriculture, with wheat acreage and hill farming, subsidies and tariffs.
These are of course only pale and petty imitations of the bolder
sweep of Hitler's or Mussolini's or Stalin's 'planning', but they
are of the same character and spring from the same origin. From
such administration, and from the increasingly elaborate surveys
on which it is based, there emerges no outline of settled law. Law
is the statesman's instrument, and it is the study proper to
humanists. The objects of administration may all, within a reasonable margin of error, be, indeed, conceived as *things*, as bricks and
milk, or even teeth and tonsils; but the objects of law are always
men and women, not merely mobilized in emergencies for particular tasks in which they are professionally skilled, and which the
State requires to have urgently performed, but living their whole
life from birth to death within the framework of liberties and
obligations, of contract and personal status, allowed or prescribed
by the lawgiver and covenanted for by the citizen. Government
by interims is always bad government; it is possible for multiplied
legislation, whether by Act of Parliament or dictatorial decree, to
destroy the very conception of law.

CHAPTER 4

Democracy and law

The judicial process: repudiation of settled law; courts of law as agencies of political education – The legislative process: identification of executive and legislative; constitutional pattern of 'spontaneous' election; failure of this pattern to create effective national parliaments – The executive process: the Bureau of the legislature; the French revolutionary search for a democratic executive before Napoleon.

I

Thus far, we have studied democracy as a religious faith, and our study has led us to contrast democratic mysticism with the European tradition of Law. That, of course, is not surprising; in all religions, the relation between faith and law is one of the central points of tension (of 'dialectic', in the language of Marxism). The earliest Christianity, with all its sacramental teaching, would make no terms with the mystery cults of its day; in its revolt from Jewish legalism, it yet identified its final enemy as 'the Lawless One'. But we must now proceed to examine democratic law more directly, as a matter of political philosophy and governmental practice.

In the logic of popular sovereignty it stands to reason that patriotism, however conceived, can be bounded by no law. Law is the command of a sovereign,[1] but there has never been any lawful sovereign save the people and, until a people has been fused into unity, it cannot exercise its sovereignty. Even when

---

[1] Is it necessary, even today, to justify this statement? The 'Law of Nature' is, of course, not Law, but a pattern to which, ideally, law should conform. The English common law is not a spontaneous emanation from a 'folk'; at no time has it had any validity in courts of law except as the command of the sovereign authority of the day.

fusion has been achieved, a sovereign people must not allow its own decrees of yesterday to limit its freedom to meet the needs of today. Old fixed law was an usurpation; new fixed law would be an abdication. Thus the incompatibility of unmixed democracy with settled law, which Aristotle detected as its chief vice, has become, in the eyes of the dogmatists of popular sovereignty, its fundamental virtue. In the language of 1789, the people must indeed, love justice, but justice itself can only be an intuition, an instinctive emotion, a personal illumination, the dictate of a 'revolutionary conscience'. At the trial of Louis XVI in December 1792 Robespierre, the lawyer, told the Convention: "You are not judges, you are and can be only statesmen." In that particular context, he was obviously right; but, in the logic of popular sovereignty, his advice must be applied to the judgment of all causes even remotely affecting public policy or social welfare; and, as the totalist tendencies of democracy develop, all conceivable causes come to partake of that character. Hence the methods of 'justice' with which we have become too familiar in Europe in recent years. "In our State" wrote the Public Prosecutor of the Soviet Union in 1938,

there is and can be no place for freedom of speech . . . for the foes of socialism. Every sort of attempt on their part to use to the detriment of the State – that is, to the detriment of all the workers – the freedoms granted to the workers must be classified as a counter-revolutionary crime.[1]

This restriction of the field of normal law is of course increased in Communist democracy by the abolition of private capital and, in all democracies, by the suppression of corporate franchises and freedoms, as being clearly incompatible with the principle of equality and as interrupting the free sweep of the sovereign people's power. In the language of 1790–1,

---

[1] Vyshinski. *The Law of the Soviet State*. Translation by H. W. Babb. Macmillan, New York, 1948.

the abolition of every kind of corporation formed among citizens of the same State is a fundamental basis of the French constitution. . . . The National Assembly abolishes irrevocably all institutions which have been injurious to liberty and equality of rights. . . . There are no longer any guilds, or corporations of professions, of arts, or of trades. . . . The law will no longer recognise monastic vows . . . consequently such vows are and shall remain suppressed in France, nor shall any such be established in future.

So far was this distrust of corporations carried that, while the law of December 14th, 1789 laid down that the new municipalities which it created should be responsible for the management of their communal property, the policy of successive governments between 1792 and 1796 was to enforce the division and enclosure of communal lands.[1]

But, within the narrowing field thus left for the operation of normal law, the judicial system of democracies does not, at first sight, seem to differ widely from that of parliamentary governments. The men of 1789 and 1918 both based the judiciary upon popular election, and the term of office of judges under the Soviet constitution of 1936 is no more than three years for courts of first instance and five for higher courts; but all this does not differ greatly from the practice of many American States, and the principles of judicial independence and irremovability except for misconduct are by none more loudly proclaimed than by official Soviet writers.[2] At least at the outset of the democratic experi-

---

[1] A new kind of corporation law has grown up in the Soviet State regulating the relations between collectivized industries, which are treated as distinct public corporations. This, however, appears to be little more than an administrative expedient; the courts are brought in to assist the State executive in the efficient management of the multifarious enterprises which it owns; the correction of abuses is more certain if their perpetrators can be sued in the courts than if their detection is left wholly to the police and Party informers.

[2] e. g. Vyshinsky. *Op. cit.* "Only the Soviet court, the court of the entire toiling people of the Soviet Union, is truly independent in the authentic and direct sense of the word." Soviet writers are, of course, bound to insist that no fact in a social democratic State *can* be identical with the same fact in a

ment, the only significant differences in the French revolutionary practice appear to have been a distrust of strict rules of evidence, as interfering with the 'spontaneous' illumination or conscience of judge and jury, and a similar distrust of professional lawyers, as exhibited in the abolition of notaries and the suppression of law schools.

When, however, we come to the most recent stage of the democratic experiment, we find in Russian legal principles what looks like a wholly different conception of law – the conception indicated by Article 3 of the Judiciary Act of 1938:

> By all their activities, the courts shall educate the citizens... in the spirit of devotion to the Motherland and the cause of Socialism, in the spirit of strict and undeviating observance of Soviet laws, of care for Socialist

---

'bourgeois' State. This makes it extraordinarily difficult to extract mere objective fact from any Soviet writing. Thus Vyshinsky argues that the Soviet system of attaching two lay assessors to each 'permanent' judge, to form a court, is more democratic than the 'bourgeois' jury system, because these assessors are elected in precisely the same way as the judge and for the same term of office. He quotes, however, with approval the Party programme of 1936 which advocated "the participation in the court of *temporary* court assessors, *constantly replaced*" (our italics), and he emphasizes that the purpose of the lay assessor system is largely to enable the maximum possible number of ordinary citizens to participate in the administration of justice. It would probably be wrong to deduce logically from this argument that the 'permanent' judges are as unlikely to secure re-election at the end of their term as the lay assessors; but in what sense they are in practice permanent, during good behaviour, and therefore in the ordinary sense independent, it is impossible to say. Indeed, even to ask the question would seem impertinent to a Russian socialist, for to him what matters is not the fact, but the idea behind it. The sovereign people – that is, the workers – expect that a judge should be independent; therefore he *is* independent, whatever may be the apparent changes and chances of his professional life. More fundamentally, perhaps, as we have suggested on page 42, an official's interior freedom from class prejudice is, to the Russian socialist, so much more important than his freedom from exterior censures, or his security of tenure in his office, that 'independence' takes on a moral, rather than a political, meaning. The analogy between this language and the language of early Christianity is obvious; deliverance from the bondage of sin was more real to the slave than any emancipation from his service to a legal master.

property, of labour discipline, of honesty towards State and social duty, of respect for the rules of Socialist Community life.[1]

This idea of the law as an educational agency bids fair to give to Soviet justice, at all levels and in all types of causes, the character of English or American Juvenile Court procedure. It is not primarily concerned, either in criminal or civil cases, with the ascertainment of facts, and, on those facts, with the infliction of penalties, or the award to the litigant of his legal rights; its concern is with the character of the criminal or the civil litigant, as revealed by the evidence, not merely about his acts, but even more, about himself. And, in this context, 'evidence' must include inference and, indeed, every shade of personal opinion. The accused's 'personality' must be 'evaluated'; his 'orientation' must be considered. In civil causes judgment must not be confined to the issue before the court, but to the whole situation between the litigants.

Of course, this idea of justice is not surprising. It is merely Fichte in practice, for, if the purpose of the State is to educate the rudimentary citizen into 'pure manhood', the court of law must be no less bound than any of the other processes of government to act primarily as a teacher. Indeed, the idea goes much farther back than that, to the earliest origins of justice in the 'dooms' of primitive judge-lawgivers sitting under a village tree or at the city gate. What our fathers regarded as the progress of civilization from 'doom' to 'law' – from *themis* to *nomos* – has been based on the postulate that adult citizens can be held responsible for their acts, and possess personal rights which they can ascertain and on which they can rely. But that postulate vanishes as soon as the adult citizen is regarded as the still imperfectly socialized member of a sovereign body, who must go back to school that he may be

---

[1] Quoted from H. J. Berman. *The Challenge of Soviet Law*. Reprinted from The Harvard Law Review, vol. 62. Nos. 2 and 3. Harvard Law Review Association.

're-orientated' towards his unfulfilled corporate duties. This new-old idea is attractive to many Western social-ists who, while not holding the dogmas of democracy, have been taught by psychologists to take the idea of adult responsibility with many grains of salt. They find a paternal form of justice, intent on 'social re-adjustment', rather than on rights or punishments, infinitely preferable to the majestic impartiality of Western law, so careful of the facts that can be proved according to nicely calculated rules, and of the classification of these facts under the categories of written law, but so apparently indifferent to the persons to whom the facts relate. They are sceptical when old-fashioned jurists remind them that Western law may be more humane precisely because it is made for men and women who are assumed to be responsible for their own lives and who have, therefore, a right not to have their lives submitted to the roving inspection of governments. Here, we are not concerned to judge this conflict of tastes; we are concerned only to identify the origins and the nature of two distinct sets of ideas, and to suggest that even the most benevolent social-ism may find it difficult to mix them.[1]

2

For most of us who are not lawyers and have had, in our own persons, only a nodding acquaintance with courts of law, it is when democracy passes from the interpretation and application

---

[1] An English jurist would, of course, deny even the analogy we have drawn in passing between Soviet law and the procedure of English Juvenile Courts. He would point out that these Courts are no less limited than any other Court to the ascertainment of the truth of a specific charge according to strict rules of evidence. The apparent analogy exists only because the vast majority of cases in the Juvenile Court begin with a plea of guilty and the proceedings of the Court are thus usually concerned, not with conviction, but with sentence. It is at that stage alone that enquiries as to character and environment are permissible under English procedure, whereas in Russia they appear to be regarded as equally relevant in arriving at a judgment of conviction or acquittal.

of old law to the making and enforcement of new law that its peculiar attitude to law becomes most clear. Broadly speaking, democracy can tolerate no distinction between executive and legislature. Both are the organs of the same General Will, which must have free course in both. To Marx, the virtue of the Commune of 1871 was that it was 'a working, not a parliamentary body, executive and legislative at the same time'. It follows that democracy in action can maintain no real distinction between legislation and executive decree, between the function of determining the principles of social life and that of responding to the expediencies of the moment. As Louis XVI complained in his Manifesto, on the occasion of his flight to Varennes in 1791, even the National Assembly of that day, though nominally a legislature committed to the old doctrine of the Separation of Powers, –

transgresses constantly the bounds which it has prescribed for itself; it concerns itself with matters related solely to the internal administration of the Kingdom and of justice, and thus engrosses all powers to itself; through its Committee of Inquisition it even exercises a despotism more barbarous and intolerable than any recorded in history.[1]

The development of such a 'total' government, if it does not spring 'spontaneously' from a popular rising, begins with the formation of a legislature in the image of the General Will. But the General Will can be expected to manifest itself only in assemblies of a size capable of expressing it with the necessary 'spontaneity'. Election must therefore be indirect, by successive tiers of electoral colleges. The men of 1789 fixed, as the ideal size for the primary electoral assembly, a maximum of 600 and a minimum of 450 members. Even the commune, the basic local unit of administration, must elect its officers in two or more sectional assemblies, if its total population exceeded 4000.

Here the logic of popular sovereignty approaches a dilemma.

---

[1] Is it fanciful to regard Senator McCarthy as a modern example of this besetting sin of democratic legislatures?

If the people act most surely when they act most directly, the moral authority of the supreme national legislature will constantly tend to be weaker than that of the primary assemblies which originate the process of national elections. No doubt this was why the men of 1789 chose as the unit of their primary electoral assemblies an artificial *Canton* which was not itself a unit of local government. They could, therefore, prescribe that the primary assemblies should have no function but that of election and should be dissolved as soon as they had discharged that function. But immediately below the Canton in the hierarchy of local areas was the *Commune* which was the basic unit of direct government by the people. Here the general assembly of electors, or its sectional assemblies, could be re-convoked at any time on the demand of 150 electors for any purpose. It has been said, with much truth, that, under the constitution of 1791, France was, in effect, a loose confederation of 40,000 communes.

The commune was, in fact, the real unit of popular sovereignty, where alone Rousseau's pattern of active citizenship could, in some sort, be realized. It was not surprising therefore that the national legislature became, from the earliest days of the Republic, the creature of the Commune and the Sections of Paris. Indeed, the most clearly marked feature of the French Revolution was the consistent unpopularity and evanescence of successive national legislatures. They commanded no loyalty and earned no respect. The truth is that an elected legislature is the worst possible mirror of the General Will of a sovereign people, because it inevitably represents contradictory schools of thought and sectional interests, and its debates must seem a constant mockery of the national unity which it claims to embody.

And, indeed, the realities of pure democracy, even in the mid-twentieth century, have remained locked up in its local units of government. Friendly critics of the Soviet system claim that in the traditional British sense of local self-government, there is in the

U.S.S.R. probably a higher degree of democracy than in most other countries.[1]

But, after all, the whole problem of politics since the beginning of recorded history has been how to translate the pre-historic tradition and practice of village self-government into terms of the larger unit of the State. The Soviet system has added the factory and the farm to the village and the town as units of local self-government, but, if pure democracy has got no farther than this, the pure democrat can only confess that he has posed the old problem in a new, and peculiarly difficult, form, and after a century and a half, has failed to solve it. Rejecting older solutions, which have had at least some measure of success, he has not yet found a new one. He is still at the stage of the New England 'town meeting' which was old when Marx was born. He has preached as a gospel, first nationalism, then internationalism, but has failed to construct even a national legislature which can either satisfy his principles, or command popular respect.

3

But success or failure in solving this age-old problem cannot be judged by this test alone. Under no system of government is any legislature, in and by itself, a satisfactory organ of constructive statecraft. Its value consists in its power to maintain, while keeping within bounds, an efficient executive; for government is not deliberation, but executive action. Even coherent legislation is possible only under executive guidance, for no deliberative body can be expected to evolve, out of itself, a consistent policy and to persevere in it athwart successive elections. And it is by this test that the French Revolution failed. No national development of the quite distinct virtues of legislation and administration, and no effective marriage between the two, is possible on a theory which asserts that the two are exactly the same. The history of the

---

[1] Schlesinger. *The Spirit of Post-war Russia*. Dennis Dobson Ltd., 1947.

decade 1789–99 is the history of a people in search of an executive government.

Its first failure in that search, under the constitution of 1791, is not to be laid wholly at the door of democratic theory, for the constitution was a compromise with a distrusted monarchy. The democratic significance of that constitution lay in its multiplication of local elected authorities and in the pattern it prescribed for local executive action in the commune, the district and the department. In each case, the executive was to be a standing committee of the local 'administrative assembly' – a 'bureau' of one-third of its members in the commune, a 'directory' of nine in the district and the department. Its officers were, for the most part, elected by the same electoral assembly as its members. When the Republic was established, the same pattern evolved itself, almost spontaneously, in the National Convention. Its parents, the National and Legislative Assemblies, had already spawned a multitude of committees, including something like a central committee for the detection of abuses; but now there came a concentration of power in the hands of one or two such bodies. In so far as France had a recognizable executive in the three years 1792–5, it was the Committee of Public Safety of the Convention.

This is, save in one respect, almost the identical pattern of the Russian Constitution of 1936: a Supreme Soviet for legislation, holding two short sessions a year and electing a standing Presidium and a Council of People's Commissars, which together constitute the supreme executive. The significant difference is that the meetings of the Supreme Soviet, though regular, are still to be only occasional. In the first eighteen years of revolutionary government, its predecessor, the All-Union Congress of Soviets, had met only seven times. A brief convocation twice a year, as at present,[1] is an interesting advance on that precedent; but only

---

[1] How far the provisions of the Constitution have been carried out in this respect, we do not know.

once, outside France, has democracy attempted to repeat the French revolutionary experiment of allowing an elected legislature to occupy in its own person the centre of the stage of government.[1] That once was Germany's Weimar Constitution of 1918, and that attempt, which we shall have to examine later, spectacularly confirmed the experience of the French Revolution.

For the solution of 1792–5 did not end the French people's search for an executive. A committee of a legislature is essentially no stronger than the legislature itself; it will be controlled and harried by the same factions which plague its parent body. The Committee of Public Safety has won a deserved renown as an emergency war executive, creating for this purpose its own extra-constitutional machinery of administration for the control of its armed forces and for the suppression of disaffection, real or supposed, in the provinces. Its success in this field has obscured both its own inherent unfitness for the normal tasks of national administration and the lack of any machinery by which it could have performed those tasks. For the essential vices of the constitution of 1791 remained, as accurately summarized in another passage of the King's Manifesto in that year:

Internal administration is entirely in the hands of the departments, districts and municipalities, . . . all elected by the people and independent of the government. . . . On the one hand, they have no favours to expect from the government; on the other, the methods provided by law for punishing or correcting their mistakes are so complicated as to be available only in extraordinary cases. The supervision of these bodies by ministers is thus reduced to a trifle.

This multiplication of elected authorities was directly dictated by democratic theory, and until the theory could be modified, the search for a national executive must continue to be frustrated. We

---

[1] The exception to this generalization is the peculiar one of the Swiss Constitution. Turkey may be on the way to becoming a second exception.

need not linger over the last and worst experiment of the Revolution, the Directory of 1795–9. From that nadir, the French people were rescued by Napoleon. There ended their search, and there began a new democratic discovery: the discovery of the plebiscitary dictatorship.

CHAPTER 5

Democracy and power. The party and plebiscite

The Party as democracy's agent of national 'spontaneity' – American and British parties – The French revolutionary experiment: the National Guard and the Jacobin Club; the club or the cell as the agent of empire – The plebiscitary executive from Napoleon to Stalin.

I

Napoleon's contribution to the democratic experiment cannot be fully understood without some further examination of the point reached by that experiment before his appearance.

In the last chapter we tried to sketch the typical constitutional pattern of a pure democracy. But the attempt is, to some extent, illusory, for the very idea of a constitution is essentially repugnant to the pure democrat. Regarding, as he must, all fixed law as an abdication by the people of its sovereign discretion, he must especially repudiate a category of law which claims to be fundamental and, therefore, specially fixed in relation to the general legal framework, If, as we have seen, every French revolutionary legislature rapidly grew unpopular, their unpopularity was greatest when they addressed themselves to constitution-making. In the winter of 1789–90 the National Assembly's reputation fell abruptly as soon as it began seriously to act as a constituent assembly; the Convention, attempting the same task in 1794–5, trembled constantly on the verge of violent dissolution; the Assembly of 1848–51 constituent from the beginning, hardly enjoyed any moment of popularity and ended in disaster. For the democrat there can be, strictly speaking, no constitutional problem, but only a problem of power; and the problem of power is not how to distribute it, but how to concentrate it. All democratic constitutions, therefore, are provisional; they merely record the point reached, at a particular moment, in the concentration of power. In Lenin's words, they "express the present correlation of forces in the class struggle". Liberals may construct a monarchy, like the last monarchy of Spain, which shall reign 'by the grace of God and the constitution'; but a democratic Louis XVI can reign only 'by the grace of God and the will of the Nation' – and that will can change. The doom of such a monarchy was spoken by the Commune of Paris on the night of August 9–10, 1792: "When the people puts itself in a state of insurrection, it withdraws and resumes all its powers".[1]

We have seen that the dilemma of democracy lies in the choice it has to make between on the one hand, a national unit of government, large enough to give the necessary scope to political and economic policy in the modern world, and, on the other hand, the small local unit in which alone the General Will may be supposed genuinely to express itself. If we view this dilemma as a constitutional problem, the solution might appear to lie in federation. That was probably Rousseau's own solution, bred, as he had been, in the atmosphere of Swiss cantonal federalism; and we may be surprised that, to the French Jacobin, constitutional federalism was always the worst of heresies. But if we view the dilemma as a problem of power, we can see that federation is, in truth, no solution at all, since, *pro tanto,* it merely removes the most important departments of policy a little further beyond the direct

---

[1] Of course, any written constitution must be provisional, in the sense that it should be broad enough to permit change, not only by amendment, but by re-interpretation. "The Constitution of the United States," said Justice O. W. Holmes, "does not enact Mr Herbert Spencer's Social Statics." But there is all the difference in the world between such prudent flexibility and pure democracy's habit of treating a constitution as if it were no more permanent than an election programme, or a record of past programmes achieved.

control of a sovereign people, and makes them rather less dependent upon that people's General Will. In terms of power, some other means must be found of transmitting, as it were, to a distance, but still directly, the heat of the General Will, without subjecting it to the cooling processes of a regular representative system. The means of transmission evolved by democracy, after many experiments, is the Party.

2

If we are to get the Single Party of democracy in its right perspective, it is useful first to compare it with the party system of the United States. The United States, as we have seen at the outset of our argument, is not a democracy in the sense in which we are using that term. Its tradition is, indeed, a passionate belief in 'government by the people', but balanced by a hardly less passionate sense of individual liberty and the rule of law. It has, however, many of the features of a pure democracy, in particular three: a multiplicity of elected assemblies and elective offices, judicial or executive; a set of wholly inadequate executives holding office for short terms; and an extreme contrast in size between the Federal unit, to which the citizen's allegiance is due, and the local units in which alone one could expect any natural sense of community to take root. In such a polity, national union cannot be created by the mere machinery of federal representative government; a national electorate, capable of getting itself intelligibly represented, has to be organized out of the multiple and, so to speak, primitive electorates of township and city. National union of this kind has been the achievement of the two American Parties and, for that achievement, many of their sins of method may perhaps be forgiven them.[1]

---

[1] Compare H. L. Stimson's speech, January 1911, on 'the present inefficiency of our State governments'; "Fear of such tyranny as some of the Royal Governors exercised over their colonies before the Revolution, was

Their method has been, in essence, the winning of votes on local issues, in order that they may be delivered as blocks of safe Party votes on State and national issues. Unhappily, local issues are often corrupt issues. In a country without a poor law, votes can be bought, indirectly and almost venially, by assistance to helpless immigrants, and it is easy to go on from that to favours in the allocation of local contracts or arrangements for immunity from police interference. It is easier still to get votes by manipulating executive patronage. It is a far cry from a New England town meeting or a Middle West Main Street to Congress and the President in Washington; but the appointment of a postmaster in Main Street or a customs collector at Salem lies with the party-elected authorities in the national capital who will listen to the party managers.

Such are the rudiments of this kind of political education; but jobbery and log-rolling are creeping sores; more and more appetites have to be satisfied, more and more tongues must be silenced; and cumulative blocks of corruption tend thus to be handed on, with the growing blocks of votes, all the way up the Party ladder. In a nation prone to violence, corruption leads easily to crime. The scale on which these evils may develop in great cities has been a common tale of scandal for nearly a hundred years. But, through all these scandals, the end of national union is being achieved; local issues, like the extension of slavery or the

---

allowed to colour and influence a situation which was entirely different. They cut the Executive down to a term too short to carry through any constructive policy; they took away his chiefs of departments and made them either elective or otherwise independent of him; they separated him as far as possible from the representative law-making body with which he must work, and in every way they reduced him to a mere ornament of doubtful beauty. . . . For a long time the only result of our faulty organization . . . was to develop a professional political class which ran our government for us. The boss and his power is the direct outgrowth of depriving the public officer of his power." *On Active Service in Peace and War.* Henry L. Stimson and Mr George Bundy. Harper Brothers, New York.

price of grain, come to be recognized as national issues of emancipation or currency reform; until, eventually, national issues, like those of peace or war, become more vivid than local issues. At that point, the Party machines have done their work and can confine themselves to their normal party function under a parliamentary constitution: the presentation of fit candidates to the electorate. If they do not take that modest course, they will find themselves perpetuating a system of corruption and crime for its own sake, without any half-redeeming national purpose.[1] For a party caucus can never be more than a makeshift agency of national union; it is, at best, a necessary evil in a country where a people is called on to govern itself before it is ready to do so.

The outstanding characteristic of the two American parties, without which they could not have done their unifying work, is that they are comprehensive parties, each embracing almost the widest possible range of political belief from 'right' to 'left', and preaching no distinctive political gospel.[2] In this, they contrast sharply with the Single Party of a democracy, whose only reason for existence is the preaching of a gospel. In order to get this aspect of democracy, too, in its right perspective, it may be useful to consider an English analogy: the twin organs of the Labour Movement, the Labour Party and the Trade Union Congress. The two are not identical and often differ in policy, but they may be conveniently treated as one for our present purpose. They are the organs of something like a 'total' movement, political,

---

[1] Or rather, perhaps, such a system, born of politics, may persist and grow almost independently of politics, as a highly profitable form of 'big business'. This seems to be the latest phase of organized crime in America. It infects politics, as any big business may infect politics; suitable judges must be elected or bought, and so on. But politics is no longer the source of the disease. The disclosures of the Senate Committee of which Senator Kefauver was chairman lie, therefore, outside our study.

[2] That is, since 1865 or so, when the slavery and 'Union' issues had been settled. One should, perhaps, except also the period of the 'nineties when 'free silver' and 'high tariff' became almost distinctive party issues.

E

social and industrial, with its own distinctive principles and its
own strict discipline. It is almost a 'proletarian' movement, and
its purpose is, not to unify a nation, but to capture a nation's
government, central and local, for the realization of its principles.
For that purpose it has, almost for the first time in the history of
the country, organized local and national elections as integral
parts of one party system. In some local areas, such as Durham
County, it has frankly used local government patronage for
party purposes and has come very near to substituting a local
party caucus, based upon miners' lodges, for the statutory local
authority as the centre of local government. But, in a country
where the national parliament has no patronage and all national
executive patronage is restricted by an independently recruited
Civil Service, such local abuses have little opportunity to spread
upwards; and though, in the emotional decade after the first
world war, the Trade Union Congress may have toyed with the
idea of becoming a revolutionary counter-government, the
Movement is now strictly constitutional, not merely from tactical
motives, but from settled conviction. Its most ominous tendency
has been to bring, not only politics and economics, but education
and all voluntary social activities within its own exclusive
organization; but this 'total' tendency, clearly marked in Miners'
Welfare Centres and in the relation of some Unions to the Central
Labour College, has hitherto been kept in check by the rooted
English distrust of all claims to 'total' power.

These two examples show that the democratic Single Party
is not peculiar in acting as a chief agency for building up the
unity of a sovereign people or for organizing and disciplining such
a people into a fighting movement. In fact, the description of the
Communist Party of the U.S.S.R. in the constitution of 1936 as
"the vanguard of the workers in their struggle for strengthening
and developing the socialist system, and . . . the leading nucleus
of all organizations of the workers" would fit well enough the

claims made by many parties in constitutional countries. But the fact remains that all such parties are dangerous, in direct proportion as they represent or serve the ideal of pure democracy. The large electorates of universal suffrage can be organized only by using a technique of enthusiasm which may be more dangerous than a mere technique of corruption. They always create the possibility of extra-constitutional and therefore irresponsible, forms of power, for it is always easier to rise to the non-parliamentary leadership of a party than to high office in a parliamentary State. And to many men party boss-hood is more attractive than official ministerial power.

Moreover, the language of a constitution is apt to express the respectabilities of a situation rather than its realities. For the realities behind the wording of the Soviet constitution, we must trace the growth of the democratic Single Party from its origins in 1789–90.

3

It began with two events: the creation of the National Guard by the decree of August 10, 1789: and the emergence in the following winter of the Jacobin Club, at first under the title of the *Amis de la Constitution*.

The National Guard was, by constitutional definition, 'not a military body, nor a State institution', but 'the citizens themselves summoned to the service of the public power'.[1] In other words, it was the sovereign people under arms; and, as such, had its own electoral machinery for the appointment of its officers. Its unit was the commune, and no officer could command a wider area than a district. It was forbidden to 'deliberate', and it could only be called out by the commune; but as every communal elector was enrolled in it, these prohibitions made little sense. In time of revolution and anarchy, how could the sovereign people

---

[1] Constitution of 1791.

more effectively assemble or deliberate than with arms in their hands? Such prohibitions could only set the Guard, in its almost inevitable activities, outside the constitution. As it was, by definition, a para-military force, so it was bound to become a para-political and para-executive power.

And, in fact, as early as October 1789 the Guard became the extra-constitutional agent of a movement which no constitutional body had any authority to inaugurate. This was the movement of the so-called 'federations', the enthusiastic fraternizations between different communes and even provinces. Thus, on February 15, 1790, such a 'federation' was established between Brittany and Anjou at Pontivy by the "solemn declaration that we are neither Angevins nor Bretons, but citizens of the same empire". The next move was to summon the *fédérés*-representatives of the Guards thus locally 'federated' – to an annual fête at Paris.

This whole movement of national unity was innocent enough in its beginnings and remained so for some two years. During that period, the Guard itself was hardly a revolutionary force; created to maintain order, it fulfilled that task, at least in the provinces, with some efficiency. Unhappily, it is almost an invariable rule that all extra-constitutional power deteriorates; a chartered irresponsibility in the exercise of unofficial power is too much for human virtue. By September 1791 it had become necessary to remind the National Guard, in the King's Proclamation of September 28, that

it was for the protection of person and property, for tax collection, and for the distribution of grain and foodstuffs, that the arms you carry were put into your hands.

Less than a year later, the *fédérés* were to enter Paris in the summer of 1792 as a chief instrument in the overthrow of the monarchy.

This deterioration was mainly the work of the Jacobin Club.

At first it was one among many party clubs, and not the most extreme; but it was the first to affiliate like-minded societies in the provinces and to organize new ones. By August 1790 some sixty provincial societies were

performing the functions of committees of inquisition, inspectors of municipalities and censors of the opinions of the citizens;[1]

by June 1791, the King could state, not unfairly, that such societies had been established

in almost all cities and even in several townships and villages, banning the existence of any other society not affiliated to themselves, deliberating on all the affairs of government, corresponding with each other on all subjects, making and receiving denunciations, bill-posting decrees, and assuming such a dominant position that almost all administrative and judicial bodies, including even the National Assembly itself, are obedient to their orders.

Most significant of all was the statement of Camille Desmoulins in February 1791 that the Club was "not only the Grand Inquisitor . . . but appears to act as the public ministry in relation to the National Assembly". Politics abhors a vacuum; if a nation tries to dispense with a constitutional executive, it will find itself ruled by a self-appointed one.

It is this assumption of executive power, and the corresponding claim to sole power, that distinguishes the democratic Single Party. It cannot be said to usurp power; it merely makes good that absence of regular power which is almost dictated by the democratic faith; it enables the local Soviet (to use the later phrase) to express itself on the national plane with the same warmth that characterizes its deliberations in the village or the factory. For the Club had its own heating system, its own methods of simulating 'spontaneity'. "The enthusiasm of the people", wrote the Duke of Wellington in 1811,

---

[1] Mercure de France August 28, 1790.

is very fine and looks well in print; but I have never known it to produce anything but confusion. In France, what was called enthusiasm was power and tyranny, acting through the medium of popular societies.

Moreover, the Club, being outside the law, could widen the boundaries of the nation without, or at least in advance of, the tiresome expedient of annexation. On the frontiers of the Austrian Netherlands and along the Rhine, the local Club, following just behind the Army or even skirmishing ahead of it, could create new communes and 'federate' them into the body of the Republic, without prematurely running the risk of diluting the national assembly of France with representatives of alien people. Later, they might be incorporated, either into France or into a separate republic of their own. The 'empire' of France – that phrase which became significantly current as the Revolution proceeded – could be thus extended like a wall-paper, for it had no closed design, but only an indefinitely repetitive pattern. We can see the same pattern of imperialism today in the western advance of Russian sovietism.

Unfortunately, the Club had no closed design either. In the absence of a dogmatic creed more settled than democracy could produce before Marx, an organization outside the law must be formless; its unity can be no more than a unity of sentiment, too weak to withstand the competitive ambition of its members. In the successive Purges of 1793-4, the Jacobins destroyed themselves in destroying their 'factions', foreshadowing, at a distance of 140 years, the later purges of the Nazi and Communist Parties in the 1930's. But, unlike the twentieth century German and Russian States, France had still no effective national executive and after five years of anarchy the Jacobin Club was revived in 1799 a few months before Napoleon's *coup d'état*.

4

Napoleon's way of reconciling popular sovereignty with a strong executive had a deadly logic in it. Let the sovereign people embody their will to action, not in a system of constitutional law, nor in a variety of extra-constitutional bodies, but in one man elected thereto, not once for all, but periodically as that man's purposes develop and as he re-submits them afresh to the people's judgment. The vital words here are 'as he re-submits them'. It is not enough to have a Presidential election every four years, as in the United States, through the ordinary electoral machinery of the nation; there must be a special and intimate relation between the sovereign people and its Chief Magistrate, in which initiative shall lie with the Chief Magistrate. If that be assured, the revolutionary machinery of ordinary elections can be allowed to continue, subject only to the supervision of the Chief Magistrate's executive officers. His almost mystic communion with the people, celebrated on crucial occasions – five times in Napoleon I's sixteen years of power, three times in Napoleon III's nineteen – replaces the haphazard enthusiasm of revolutionary 'spontaneity'. Such a chief magistrate will be, not only a supreme executive, but in the logic of popular sovereignty, the supreme incarnation of the people. "Do you represent the people?", asked Napoleon I in his famous outburst to members of the *Corps Legislatif* on January 1, 1814, "I am its representative. Four times I have received the votes of five millions of citizens. I have a right to speak and you have none. You are merely delegates of the departments."

Even a plebiscite, however, is a poor expression of this mystic communion. If it were possible, it would be better that the communion should be bound to no forms, that the Chief Magistrate should simply emerge before his people, as a new Pope emerges from the Conclave, and that, like the Pope, he should thereafter exercise a universal authority, not by virtue of any identifiable form of control over the machinery of government, but by virtue of his own personal infallibility. Hitler came near to realizing this dream, and Stalin seems actually to have realized it.[1]

---

[1] I leave the following passage as I originally wrote it in 1952.

In the constitutional discussions of 1935, he resisted proposals to complete the constitution by providing for a plebiscitary President of the Union of Soviet Republics. Having refused that offer of a crown, he still holds no State office. The constitutional election of 1936 may perhaps be regarded as his plebiscite, but he hardly required this confirmation, and in what could it confirm him? He has simply emerged from the Party and has blessed his people, who have knelt and applauded. If his successor were successfully to emerge in the same way, the result might be the apotheosis of the Party rather than the apotheosis of the plebiscitary dictatorship. But, meanwhile, he represents, for the moment, the culmination of the mystic communion between one supreme man and the sovereign people:

> He is our Path, our reason, our conscience
> When we decide for or against,
> We try to picture
> *His* smile and *his* eyes.
> The truth of the plain folk lived and lives in him.[1]

---

[1] Quoted from Maynard. *Op. cit.*

II

The movement to catastrophe
Nationalist democracy

The conclusion of the preceding chapters has been that the logic of the Democratic State has led directly to the Union of Socialist Soviet Republics. But the argument of the following three chapters is that, on its way to this Marxian goal, the Democratic State has led its devotees successively into two blind alleys. It has led France into the blind alley of a sovereign parliament; it led nearly the whole of Europe between the wars into the blind alley of nationalism. Only in Germany did nationalism assume an effective form; and there it proved disastrous. It destroyed Germany, and nearly destroyed Western Europe. According to this view, Hitler was the almost logical product of Weimar democracy, and both were the logical products of German nationalist philosophy from its beginnings in the latter half of the eighteenth century.

Western Europe is still in the grip of the democratic superstition. It has no longer any philosophy either of the State or of international law which can provide a coherent alternative to communism. What it needs is a philosophy of Dualism which can be set with conviction against the philosophy of Totalism.

CHAPTER 6

Nationalism: the German Volk

From Napoleon to Stalin via Germany – French democracy as a blind alley –
Origins of German nationalism – The necessity of nationalism in democratic
logic.

I

It is a long road from Napoleon to Stalin, and, oddly enough,
the main highway between the two does not run through the
history of France.

France is the Neanderthal Man of democracy, a first experiment
which seems to have come to a dead end. After trying two people's
republics, two plebiscitary empires and two constitutional
monarchies, she abandoned, after 1870, her search for a people's
executive, and has come to rest successively in a third and a
fourth republic, governed by a legislative assembly, in almost
continuous session, freely elected by the people, but dominated
and immobilized by competitive party groups. Under her first
post-revolutionary monarchy, a wise cross-bencher told the
parliament of that day that it had come to represent a quiet
people's lurking dislike of all settled political authority:

Anarchy, expelled from society by the need for order and repose . . .
has found a home in this Chamber. You no longer have a real majority,
united in sentiment and policy, but only a succession of illusory majorities which are, at root, no more than minorities accidentally swollen by
different and even contrary opinions. . . . There is no steady will, no
fixed and constant purpose.[1]

What Royer Collard denounced in the 1820's seems now, after
125 years, to have become the deliberate choice of a good-
hearted but profoundly sceptical people.

---

[1] Quoted from E. Spuller, *Royer Collard*, Hachette, 1895.

Such a choice may be not unnatural by such a people after such a history. It may, indeed be one of the normal dead-ends of democracy. A sovereign people who cannot find a way to express their virtues in a strong national government may, perhaps usefully, and with apparent safety, sublimate their vices in a weak one. Between 1815 and 1870, the French people certainly found it difficult to express their virtues at the national level. Some twenty years after Royer Collard's speech, when, under a new monarchy, France seemed to have found the secret of a stable parliamentary majority, another cross-bencher, de Tocqueville, told the Ministry of Guizot:

Keep the laws as they are, if you wish, though I think you will be very wrong to do so; even keep the same men in office, if that pleases you; but for God's sake change the spirit of your government, for I tell you again that the spirit you have is leading you to the abyss.

The abyss of the 1848 revolution opened, in fact, within a month of that speech, and the speaker afterwards wrote the epitaph of the same Ministry in more particular language: the government of France,

had the appearance of a business company, all whose operations were undertaken with a view to the profit which would accrue to the shareholders.

Lamartine's estimate of the situation on the eve of the revolution was more superficial: *"La France s'ennuie."* But, after the Republican fevers of 1848–9, when a second plebiscitary dictator had established what looked like a strong government, with something like an adequate programme of economic development and social welfare, only to plunge France again into the disaster of an unnecessary war – after all this, might not a people prefer to be bored?

Even plebiscitary dictatorship, though a French invention, proved a dead end in the hands of the Napoleons. The first Napoleon, his military genius apart, was a throwback to the eighteenth century, rather than a forerunner of the nineteenth and twentieth, the successor of reforming monarchies and ministers like the Emperor Joseph II, Leopold of Tuscany and Pombal in Portugal. Napoleon III confessed as much when he summed up his intentions after his *coup d'état* in 1851: "The name of Napoleon is a whole programme in itself. It means: at home, order, authority, religion, and the well-being of the people; abroad, national dignity." Frederick II of Prussia might have promised the same, if he had ever taken the trouble to translate his policy into popular terms.[1]

It is, indeed, through Germany that the main road of democracy runs, and Frederick II has some claim to be its pioneer. Marx was not quite right in thinking that a bourgeois revolution must precede a social democratic one. There is, indeed, no 'must' about historic sequences, as Lenin was to prove; but the two most favourable precedent conditions for the introduction of any form of pure democracy are a unified and efficient State and a national idea; and if these two can be combined with a strong habit of submission to authority, so much the better.

The extreme inefficiency of royal administration in eighteenth century France, coupled with her multifarious provincial privileges and autonomies and her social prides and prejudices, as it was the immediate cause of the democratic revolution, was also the reason for its ultimate failure. It was difficult to bring even equality, the one dear desire of the French people, to effective birth in a society which had so long been broken, to quote the phrase of a French historian, into a "cascade of disdain", splashing

---

[1] Even the mention of 'religion'. For this atheist had a religious policy. He believed that "the common interests of Protestant princes" should unite them in opposition to religious persecution. "In my kingdom everybody may seek salvation as suits him best". All that Frederick or either Napoleon wanted of religion was the teaching of obedience to the Head of the State; Napoleon I had to effect that by an official catechism: but in the land of Luther, Frederick could rely on the services of a submissive Church.

down all the infinite petty gradations of social rank. And as to a
national idea, France has always been to Frenchmen primarily a
land, not a people; they "do not recognize the ethnographic
argument", as Lavisse said to a German statesman in 1914: they
are more ready, like Gregoire in 1792, to "subpoena the archives
of nature" in order to fix the frontiers of their *pays*, than to call
history as a witness to their "manifest destiny" as a nation.[1]

2

Much of what France thus lacked, Prussia after 1815 possessed
and could convey to Germany; while what Prussia still lacked,
the rest of Germany could supply.

Prussia has been so long treated as the black sheep of the
European family of nations that we tend to forget her outstanding
contributions to the art of modern government: especially, the
establishment, early in the nineteenth century, of an efficient, and
on the whole an enlightened and progressive, civil service always
at the service of social welfare. In the 1840's when Chadwick, in
England, was labouring at the first beginnings of sanitary reform,
and when Guizot, in France, could make, in eight years, no better
contribution to social policy than a single law for the suppression
of child labour under eight years of age, Prussia had already set
the world a model of 'medical police' administration which is
still in advance of the practice of some European countries.
Indeed, in the reconstruction of the new territories of Prussia in
West Poland and the Rhineland after 1815, there was not a little
to justify Treitschke's boast about the "magnanimous Prussian
fashion" of respecting old local customs, while incorporating
them into a new national unity. To all this, based as it was on the
foundations laid by Frederick, Prussia could add some real sense

---

[1] The nationalism which the school of Maurras and Barrès tried to foist on
France between the wars was an artificial imitation of an envied Germany, and
proved only that all nations are liable to fits of all aberrations.

of social equality, consisting in a common loyalty to the Supreme State and in a consequent recognition of distinctions won by service in the army or the bureaucracy as more important than those derived from birth.

These Prussian achievements were, moreover, the more significant for the future because they were not the achievements of her Kings. It would be easy to compile a whole anthology of contempt, to illustrate the world's opinion of the lamentable succession of Hohenzollerns who cumbered the seventy-two years between the death of Frederick II in 1786 and the accession of William I to the regency in 1858.[1] To Prussians, looking back over that waste of years, the Great Fritz appeared in the glamour, not so much of hereditary divine right, as of personal leadership; he could easily be assimilated, along with Luther, into the future cult of a *Führerprinzip*.

Still, all this did not add up to anything that could be called a national idea, and, indeed, Prussia was to achieve German unity in the teeth of German nationalism. Bismarck's "Prussians we are and Prussians will we remain", was a faithful description of his policy. But even Bismarck could not destroy the typical German mystery cult of the *Volk*, rooted in history and developed in the enthusiasms of the War of Liberation against Napoleon. Just because German history had been a history of perpetual political frustration – because German jurists still struggled in vain to develop out of the traditional German *Volksrecht* a system of modern law which could bear comparison either with Roman law or with the Code Napoleon – the more wonderful did the persis-

---

[1] For instance: Malmesbury on Frederick William II in 1794. "This is an alliance with the Algerines, whom it is no disgrace to pay, nor any impeachment of good sense to be cheated by"; Heine on Frederick William III: "They say he is a religious man and believes in the Creed; ah! would that he believed in Jupiter who takes vengeance on the oath-breaker, and would give us at last the constitution he promised us"; Gerlach on Frederick William IV in 1855: "How can you conduct such delicate business ¦with . . . , to say no more, so incalculably queer a master?"

tence of the German *Volk* itself appear, the more easy was it to believe Fichte's eloquence when he exalted it as, in its own right, the master principle of the world. A man must be able to "find heaven already on this earth and infuse eternity into his daily work", and for this purpose

the nation is the eternal to which he entrusts his own eternal life and the eternal continuance of his work. It is the eternal order of things in which he stores his own immortality. He must determine to preserve it, for it is the only liberating medium in which the short span of his life on earth can be prolonged on earth into an enduring life.

When this people-God should be fused with Hegel's God-State, when Prussian State Schools should become the home of Fichte's nationalist education, the world, for good or ill, might indeed expect to see a new birth.

And the new birth was likely to reproduce all the essential lawlessness of pure democracy. For, into the cult of the *Volk* had been injected, towards the close of the eighteenth century, a curious philosophical conception embodied in a characteristic German phrase. In one of his most rhetorical rhapsodies, Fichte lauded the infinite potentialities of the German language. Bound by the limits of available language, he said,

the genius of other peoples can only strew with flowers the trodden roads of the ancient world, and weave decorative robes for the wordly wisdom which they lightly mistake for philosophy. But, in contrast, the German mind will open up new strata of thought, and let in light and air into their depths, and hurl up the rock-masses from which future ages will build themselves dwellings.

There really seems to be some truth in this, though not in the favourable sense that Fichte assumed. Anyway, when in 1784 a German philosopher and theologian, Herder, took over from French encyclopaedists, and from at least one Italian writer,[1] the idea of Progress, which had been making its way among European

---

[1] Vico. *Scienza nuova.*

thinkers since the beginning of the eighteenth century, he endowed it with a new German name. To him, the law of the universe and of human history was *Ewiges Werden*. The phrase is untranslatable and has an emotional force beyond the implications of mere 'progress' or 'evolution', or even 'perfectibility'. Perhaps 'perpetual emergence' would come nearest to its meaning, as thus:

The flower of humanity, captive still in its germ, will blossom one day into the true form of man like unto God, in a state of which no terrestrial man can imagine the greatness or the majesty.[1]

"No terrestrial man", but Herder's hope was a terrestrial one. It was the fore-ordained culmination of man's natural growth. The growth was not, like that of the French *philosophes,* a mere emancipation and development of the human intellect; Herder's immediate predecessor in Germany, Lessing, had foreshadowed a progressive series of religions which would yet lift man to a higher plane than that of Christianity.

Such language came to penetrate German literary and popular thought. Elsewhere, under the forms of democracy or parliamentary government, nationalism has been generally a conservative force, though often an internationally aggressive one, for it tends to draw its main inspiration from a historic past. The watchword of Mazzini's Roman Republic in 1848–9 might be "a people's Rome, the Italy of the future"[2] but, once the fervours of insurrection were past, the people were more likely to be tamed by Rome than to change her, and the future of Italy was more likely to be moulded by memories of Roman imperialism than by any novel radicalism. But once combine, in a country like Germany, a political past which its people regard as a reproach to be wiped out, rather than as a splendour to be revived, with the idea of an ancient and enduring People the law of whose being is, not mere

---

[1] Quoted from H. B. Bury: *The Idea of Progress.* Macmillan 1921. The analogy with Mazzini's "indefinite revelation" (see page 28) is obvious.

[2] *"Roma del popolo, Italia del' avvenire".*

persistence, but creative change, and the result is sure to be volcanic.

The more volcanic because of the religious implications of this version of democratic nationalism. Apart from the People there is no salvation, no guarantee of any immortality which it is worth a man's while to hope for. As in Israel of old, a man's worst fate is to be 'cut off from the people'. The analogy here is very close, for this People is a Chosen People. It is the sole trustee of the world's future, the only recipient of new religious revelations, the only constructor of habitations for mankind in future ages. Moreover, this claim to be a Chosen People was later reinforced by a curious abdication of the claims of the Christian Church to be the prime channel of a divine revelation. In the 1880's Wellhausen, the greatest of German Old Testament scholars, expressed this abdication in a startling dictum:

We must acknowledge that the Nation is more certainly created by God than the Church, and that God works more powerfully in the history of nations than in Church history.

By its very nature, be it noted, this cult of the *Volk* must become the peculiar religion of young men. They, the latest respositories of creative change, must be its high priests. From the *Burschenschaften* of the early nineteenth century to the *Wandervögel* and the other youth groups of the early twentieth, they were taught to regard themselves as the trustees of a new world in the throes of birth. Naturally, and at first almost innocently, they became the *Hitlerjugend* of unhappy memory.

3

Such was the Germany created by the nineteenth century and, consequently, nationalism, in any exact sense of that much misused word, has been, like Fichte's religion of education, a special German contribution to the development of democracy.

Outside Germany, nationalism has had no sure foundations.

Of course, any group of men long accustomed, as in Spain, to live under one government, or remembering, as in Poland, that they once so lived in what they feel to have been happier days, will unite to preserve or restore that government. Equally of course, the inhabitants of any country, like Italy, which is at least, in Metternich's contemptuous phrase, a distinct 'geographical expression', may wish to abolish frontiers and political systems which unnecessarily divide it, especially if they have a common language and a common historic past. And, further, under modern conditions of government, any group within a State possessing, like the Slovaks or the Irish, a language or a religion which is not the common possession of the whole State, may be impelled by a system of compulsory State education, or by other activities of a too busy State administration, to assert their right to home rule or to complete independence.

Up to this point, most of these natural tendencies towards unity or division might, it would seem, be satisfied without any major political change, if governments could only be tolerant, and minorities only reasonable. Hence the argument urged by Americans, like Justice Brandeis during the first World War, that nationality should be regarded as a cultural, not a political, fact. But the idea of pure democracy injects a new element into the problem: the sheer doctrinal necessity of defining the identity of the 'self-determining' popular sovereign. The identification then proceeds on the basis of mixed arguments drawn from race, language, religion, history and geography – and, if the debaters are wiser than they usually are, from the distribution of economic resources and the requirements of self-defence. But no one has ever succeeded in evolving from all these considerations anything which even looks like a political principle.

This lack of principle was fatal to the democratic revolutions of 1848 in Central Europe. Constituent assemblies in Frankfurt or Prague, wrangling over theoretical national entities, could not withstand the Austrian Empire's simple insistence on a single political fact: "Austria's continued existence as a united State is a German, as well as a European necessity."[1] The peacemakers of 1919 were to forget that thesis, only to prove its truth. The history of the seventy years between these dates reverberates with the bricks dropped by English and American statesmen in their vain attempts to speak correctly the new European language of nationalism. In 1862 Gladstone, his head full of Italian reminiscences, hailed the Southern Confederacy as 'a new nation', a phrase which must have been as strange to Jefferson Davis as it was repugnant to Seward. In 1917 Woodrow Wilson,[2] thinking probably in terms of Ireland, committed the reverse blunder when he innocently implied in the tenth of his Fourteen Points, that the "peoples of Austria-Hungary" were something less than nations and could be contented with "an opportunity of autonomous development". The confusions of the peace settlement at Versailles faithfully reflected, again, this lack of an intelligible principle of nationality. Perhaps the worst frontier drawn under it, that between Hungary and Roumania, was nearly the most defensible on grounds of race and language, and even of geography; perhaps the best, the so-called 'Curzon line' between Poland and Russia, reproduced approximately the old frontier of the First Partition of Poland which had then been based, not on geography, race or language, but on religion: the boundary between a Catholic and an Orthodox population.

It would, obviously, be too much to assert that Germany succeeded in evolving an intelligible principle out of her cult of the *Volk*, but she did succeed in generating from it, as Mazzini's Italy failed to do, a driving force, not merely for insurrection, but

---

[1] Declaration of the Kremsier Diet November 27, 1848.

[2] He used to say in conversation that a nation was like a gentleman; you could not define the term, but you knew one when you met him. This was perhaps the naïvest epigram ever perpetrated by a statesman with a historian's training.

for government. Not, of course, for settled government, as constitutionalists understand settlement, for that is unthinkable in a democracy; but one which, however changeable in form, might come to express something like the constant will and consistent sense of direction which is the postulate of popular sovereignty. It might be the better equipped for that purpose by its high tradition of executive administration – that bureaucratic idea which Max Weber, the leading German social philosopher of the early twentieth century and a father of the Weimar Constitution of 1919, had rationalized into the main foundation of his political teaching. "Socialisation", he wrote in February 1919, "is administration".[1] Here, then it seemed, was a 'people' ready-made, already politically educated and administratively equipped. At least, if a German *Volksstaat* were to fail, nationalism, too, would have to be written off as another of democracy's blind alleys.

Well, it would seem that it must be written off. The story of the German *Volksstaat* created at Weimar, is, perhaps, not yet fully told; but it had, in its two phases of parliamentary government and dictatorship, the same twenty-five years of continuous life as France's first experiment in revolutionary democracy and empire. Continuous, for Hitler had the same claim to be the fulfilment of the German revolution as Napoleon I of the French. If that was a sufficient test, there can be no doubt of its failure. But the reasons for that failure deserve some further study.

---

[1] Quoted from Scheele. *The Weimar Republic*. Faber and Faber, 1946.

CHAPTER 7

The German Volksstaat: Weimar and Hitler

The German experiment in nationalist democracy – Proportional representation – The plebiscitary presidency from Ebert to Hitler – Constitutional formulations of the Duties of Man – Identification of People and Party.

I

The outstanding characteristic of the German *Volksstaat* established at Weimar, was its authors' whole-hearted choice of the nation, as against any more local units, as the sole arena for the direct expression of the people's will. The twenty-five States of Bismarck's Federal Reich survived as mere sub-divisions of one sovereign "German people, united in all its branches".[1] As such, they were bound to the same republican form of government as the Reich. Locally, they exercised little but delegated powers; centrally, their representatives in the new *Reichsrat* had but the shadow of the authority they had enjoyed in Bismarck's *Bundesrat*. The Reich might change their boundaries without their consent, and might, through the procedure of 'execution', supersede their governments.

Below the level of the State, there were hardly any units which had been, or could become, national centres of public feeling or of self-government, or could even provide the primary basis for a system of indirect election on the French revolutionary model. Municipal government, at least in Prussia, had been too much dominated by the bureaucracy to breed any sense of active responsibility in the citizen; trade union organization had been too

---

[1] Constitution. Art. 1.

centralized and too subservient to the political preoccupations of the Social Democratic party; responsibility for social insurance against sickness, accident and old age had been centralized too exclusively in the hands of the State. Without a comprehensive change in the whole structure and traditions of German society, the German people could, therefore, only express their will at the national level, in the legislature and executive of the Reich and must express it there directly by, as it were, long-range transmission.

The Weimar fathers invited them to do so by a plebiscitary vote, every seven years, for the President of the Reich and a vote by areas, every four years, for the members of the Reichstag, under a system of pure proportional representation. The areas were very large, only thirty-five in the whole country, and the electoral machinery was designed to ensure that every 60,000 votes polled should elect one member. Nothing could, on the surface, appear more democratic, and the experiment, launched on the very eve of the introduction of broadcasting, had, it might be thought, better prospects of success than any previous device for the mobilization of the General Will of a sovereign people in a supreme democratic legislature.

Unfortunately, as the event proved, proportional representation on this scale is exactly calculated to produce strong parties and weak governments. Theoretically it is supposed to ensure the representation of all minorities large enough to muster the standard number of votes; in practice, it ensures only the representation of minority *parties* strong enough to compile and advertise a party 'list'. A geographical single-member constituency of 60,000 voters may sometimes be won by an eccentric candidate on his personality; but the lone angler cannot hope to cast his line successfully in the sea of a multiple-member region – he must join the crew of a trawler. On the other hand, there is room in such a sea for half a dozen trawlers or more. From January 1919 to March 1933, the Reich supported at least five major parties, none of whom ever commanded a majority of the Reichstag. Only the Reichstag of 1920 lasted its full four years.

Moreover, the representative of a relatively small geographical constituency can feel some real responsibility to identifiable constituents; but the fractional beneficiary of the votes collected by a party 'list' will feel responsibility only to the party. Such a party will not long refrain from controlling the actions of its members, even when – indeed, especially when – they become members of the executive government. In Weimar Germany, the existence of multiple parties compelled government by successive coalitions, and the power of the party caucuses to require the resignation of its members from the ministry made each coalition insecure. In 1929 Stresemann protested that "the 'withdrawal' of Ministers means that, in reality, the individual no longer exists, except as the nominee of a particular organisation".[1] In 1926 the Nationalist Party, with 103 members in the Reichstag out of 485, telegraphed instructions to the Chancellor, Luther, at Locarno forbidding him to sign any treaty with the Western Powers without reference to the Party. Those instructions were ignored but the incident is typical. When several parties thus seek to pull the strings of their parliamentary puppets, all the way up, so to speak, to the steps of the throne, the resulting confusion of counsels comes near to justifying Hitler's description of parliamentary politicians as the "medicine men of the white race".

2

The 'steps of the throne' is not a bad description of the supreme executive power in the Weimar *Volksstaat*. For the Weimar fathers, while determined to regulate the relations of Chancellor and Cabinet with the Reichstag according to the English model of 'responsible' government, endowed the President personally

---

[1] Quoted from Scheele. *Op. cit.*

with a combination of all, and more than all, the powers possessed by the President of the United States as Commander-in-Chief of the army and by the former German emperors as rulers by divine right. He could suspend constitutional rights and could govern by decree. True, his personal acts must be countersigned by the Chancellor or the responsible minister; true, also, that he must submit his acts *ex post facto* to the Reichstag for approval; but, in the last resort, conflicts between President and Reichstag could be settled only by a referendum to the whole people, and a referendum decided in the President's favour was equivalent to his re-election for a further period of seven years.

It is easy now to see the extreme danger of this attempt to blend two quite distinct principles of government – the academic liberalism of proportional representation and the bonapartism of strong executive power – and to assimilate them both to the ideals of pure popular sovereignty. It is easy to point out that the discretionary personal powers of an American President, as commander in chief of the army in a non-military country, are invested with much less dignity or authority than the acts of a German President, as the direct representative of the whole German people, with all the tradition behind him of European plebiscitary democracy, Prussian militarism, and German philosophy of the State and the *Volk*. It is easy, too, to wish that politicians would sometimes read the more erratic prophecies dropped in passing by literary men, such as that of an irrepressible Irishman writing, at the turn of the century, on Wagner's *Ring:*

The most inevitable dramatic conception of the nineteenth century is that of a perfectly naive hero, upsetting religion, law and order in all directions, and establishing in their place the unfettered action of Humanity, doing exactly what it likes and producing order instead of confusion thereby, because it likes to do what is necessary for the good of the race. This conception . . . was certain at last to reach some great artist and be embodied by him in a masterpiece. It was also certain that, if that master happened to be a German, he should take delight in describing his hero as the Freewiller of Necessity, thereby beyond measure exasperating Englishmen with a congenital incapacity for metaphysics.[1]

That unintended portrait of a *Führer*, drawn a quarter of a century before the first appearance of Hitler, might have given pause to Englishmen and Americans in 1919, as they demanded the dissolution of the Empire and the establishment of 'democracy' in Germany. A Hohenzollern, whatever his faults, was at least unlikely to play the part of Siegfried.

It is much less easy, however, in the comparative study of constitutions, to distinguish the Weimar pattern of government from other more orthodox patterns. For instance, the Presidential powers under Article 48 of the Weimar constitution were very like the Viceroy's and Governors' 'special powers', inserted by the British Parliament, after exhaustive consideration, in the Government of India Act of 1935. Indeed, President Ebert's government by decree and military force in the Ruhr crisis between September 26, 1923 and February 13, 1924 was pretty much of the kind contemplated, in such an emergency, by the drafters of the Indian constitution. Was it then to be wondered at that liberal-minded Germans like Prince Max of Baden should have applauded the Presidential clauses of the Weimar constitution as the solution of democracy's old problem of combining popular government with an efficient executive? Was there, after all, anything much wrong with these clauses?

The answer surely is that there was nothing much wrong with them except the basic affirmation of the constitution, in its first article, that "political authority is derived from the people". A pure democracy can protect itself against revolution or counter-revolution; but by no constitutional device can it protect itself against usurpation. And usurpation is its real risk. In normal times the throne of the people's Chief Delegate is always half-

---

[1] G. Bernard Shaw. *The Perfect Wagnerite*.

vacant, for in such times it will be filled by the most 'available' party nominee or by a non-political caretaker, who will occupy it provisionally, while the people await the coming of a fairy prince. Of all the mis-readings of history on which the British governing class were trained at the beginning of the twentieth century, the worst was, perhaps, the ridicule commonly heaped upon the principle of 'legitimacy', as propounded by Talleyrand at the Congress of Vienna. However much Talleyrand may have spoken with his tongue in his cheek; however much his phrase may have been discredited by Metternich's subsequent use of it; it embodies the most vital consideration in the whole art of politics. The chief problem of civilized government has always been to regulate, not so much the exercise of political power, as the succession to such power. Democracy, in effect, abandons that problem; it not only refuses to protect itself against usurpation but invites it and, indeed, relies upon it to solve all major issues of government.

This elementary fact was clear enough to the best public men of Germany – at least to Stresemann who, as early as 1927, made no secret of his belief that German government could be stabilized only by a Hohenzollern restoration, within the framework of a parliamentary constitution. But the idea remained anathema, not only to Frenchmen who had accustomed themselves since 1871 to associate democracy with weakness, but also to Englishmen whose traditions of constitutional monarchy might have taught them better.

3

And the usurper, when he came, slipped so easily into the place and practice of his predecessors! The republican governments of 1930 and 1931 had fallen back, in the economic crisis, on the example of government by decree set by the two Stresemann cabinets in 1923–4, on the occasion of the invasion of the Ruhr.

In 1931 55 per cent of the legislation of the Reich had been enacted by emergency decree; in 1932 93 per cent. The National Socialist legislation of 1933 was, by this standard, almost normal. The Enabling Act passed by the Reichstag in March 1933 seemed, at first sight, hardly to differ from the similar Act passed ten years earlier in October 1923. The Act of April 1933, substituting Reich regents for the State Presidents, and the Act of January 1934, abolishing the sovereignty of the States, seemed the logical consummation of the Weimar Constitution itself. The preamble to the latter Act proclaiming, on the strength of the plebiscite of November 1933, that "the German people has been blended into an indissoluble unity which has done away with all internal political barriers and differences", hardly extended the principle, already recorded in the constitution, that the German people was "united in all its branches". If von Papen, in June 1932, had subverted the government of Prussia, had not Ebert and Stresemann subverted those of Saxony and Thuringia nine years before, in strict pursuance of their constitutional powers? Of course, those constitutional powers were intended for use only in an emergency; but who could say that the world economic collapse of the 'thirties, which was forcing even the Congress of the United States to give President Roosevelt the large discretionary powers of the New Deal, was less of an emergency than the troubles of 1923–4? Only the *Volk* could judge, and their votes had left no doubt of their judgment.

If the usurper could thus find himself almost at home in "the most democratic constitution in the world", he had plenty of precedents also for the policies he would follow under that constitution. The twentieth of the 'Twenty-five Points' of the programme of the National Socialist German Workers Party, published in 1920 and republished without change in 1932, laid down that "an understanding of the theory of the State must be taught to children at the earliest possible age". But even in 1920 this demand was not materially in advance of the educational policy of the Weimar constitutionalists, with its attempt to ensure the passage of every German child, from the ages of 6 to 10, through one uniform type of State primary school, the *Grundschule*. We have seen how essential this idea had been, since the beginning of the nineteenth century, to the German conception of democracy. But if the State is to assume this exclusive responsibility for forming the mind of the people, how carefully must it select and train the teachers it employs! Only the very innocent will believe that politics played no part in the selection and training of teachers in the early Socialist days of the Weimar republic; from the practice of those days, the Civil Service Law of April 1933 differs in little except in its outspoken brutality:

Officials (including teachers both in schools and Universities) may be dismissed from service who, because of their previous political activities, do not offer surety that they will at all times act unreservedly for the national State.

More fundamentally, the Weimar constitution had made one new experiment in democracy: it had attached to its declaration of rights of the citizen a declaration also of his duties:

Every German has, without prejudice to his personal liberty, the moral duty so to use his intellectual and physical powers as is demanded by the welfare of the community;[1]

and, in regard to the citizen's right to property,

Property imposes obligations. Its use by its owner shall at the same time serve the public good.[2]

Could anything be in more impeccable accordance with the best political philosophy, as expounded, for instance, in England by T. H. Green to the Oxford generation which was to judge Weimar Germany? Yet, in fact, this balancing refinement of the Rights of Man reduced to even deeper absurdity the whole underlying

---

[1] Article 163. [2] Article 153.

fallacy of such oracular statements of general principles in the form of law. The language of law is the language of guarantee and enforcement; it knows nothing of moral rights, unenforceable save at the tribunal of conscience. At the very beginning of the European attempt to formulate fundamental rights, in August 1789, Malouet had warned the States General of the dangers of the path on which they had entered:

Why carry mankind to the top of a mountain and show them all the extent of their rights, when we are compelled to make them come down again, to assign them limits and to throw them back into the real world, where they will find themselves hedged about at every step?

But still more must it be true that law knows nothing of moral obligations. The Soviet State has, in some sort, solved the problem of constitutional declarations of rights, by confining them to what the State believes itself to have already achieved – for instance, the right to work in a collectivized State; but when it attaches to such a statement of rights, as it does, a corresponding statement of duties – for instance, the duty of 'work discipline' – it enters a field where undefined duties invite the exercise of arbitrary power:

Hence the obligation of an honourable attitude towards the social duty and discipline of work inscribed in Artical 130 of the U.S.S.R. Constitution. Against those who disorganize production and those who undermine the discipline of work, the state has established a number of criminal measures applied by the Soviet courts as dictated by the gravity and the consequences of the crime or violation.[1]

And so in Germany. Article 163 of the Weimar Constitution reappeared within a year in the tenth point of the Nazi programme:

It must be the primary duty of every citizen to engage in productive work, whether in physical or intellectual fields. The activities of individuals must not be such as to conflict with the general interest but, on the contrary, must be for the common good.

Similarly, Article 153 reappeared in the seventeenth point, in

---

[1] Vyshinsky. *Op. cit.*

language which Hitler, as early as 1928, had some difficulty in explaining away to his more conservative supporters:

We demand agrarian reform consistent with our national needs; the passage of a law to expropriate without compensation land which is to be used for common purposes; the abolition of interest on agricultural mortgages and of all speculation in land values.[1]

Of such were Hitler's debts to democracy. But he was not a mere borrower. He added one almost original contribution to democratic theory and practice: the blunt assertion that the Party *is* the People. As we have seen, democracy has always had to identify, and to adopt some restrictive definition of, the 'people', in order to produce a sovereign who would really work. Even parliamentary governments have been tempted to substitute for the people, by whose consent they profess to govern, some smaller entity like Guizot's *pays légal*, the community of responsible voters under a narrow franchise. It was perhaps Burke's greatest virtue that he armed conservative opinion in England against this temptation, so that Tory and Old Whig aristocrats accustomed themselves to resist electoral reform on the almost liberal ground that each member of parliament was already a representative, not of any technical constituency known to the law, but of the whole people. As we have seen, too, democracy's solution of this problem has been twofold: the Party and the personal dictator. But, before 1933, no democrat, not even any communist, had gone so far as actually to decree that the Party "has become the repository[2] of the government and is inseparably connected with the State". No one before had substituted the Party in Arms for the People in Arms, proclaiming the "members of the Party and

---

[1] Most of these quotations from the Constitution and the Nazi programme are taken from R. L. Buell and others, *New Governments in Europe*, published by the Foreign Policy Association. Thomas Nelson and Sons, New York, 1934.

[2] *Trägerin*. Compare Desmoulin's '*exerce le ministère public*' (page 69).

of the Storm Troops as the leading and moving power of the National Socialist State".[1] And, of course, no earlier nationalist had defined the People behind the Party in terms purely of heredity.

Only a member of our people may be a citizen. Our people are only those of German blood. Therefore, no Jew may be a member of our people. Only citizens may decide on the leadership and laws of the State.[2]

In 1934 Professor Toynbee stigmatized this theory as 'tribalism';[3] but it is worse. It is nationalism. It is the worship of humanity in the guise of the *Volk*. For that worship must have its idol or its incarnation, and the last is worse than the first. This is Fichte's 'nation made Man' – the new Man with a new morality, whose motto had been written for him by Nietzsche: "How weary am I of my Good and of my Evil".

---

[1] Law of December 2, 1933.
[2] Points 4 and 5 of the Party programme.
[3] *Survey of International Affairs*, 1933.

CHAPTER 8

Nationalist Europe between the wars

Consequences of democracy – Economic nationalism and the decline of capitalism – British policy crippled by the figment of a democratic Germany in a democratic League of Nations – Democracy as the destroyer of a rational 'system of Europe': denial of law by democracy and its exaggeration by international jurists – Need for a dualist alternative to totalism.

I

We have followed democracy down the blind alley of nationalism to its end in those 'dark places of the earth' which are 'full of the habitations of cruelty'. We have not sought to explore those habitations, because they have been the common end of so many other blind alleys of lawless power; it would be hardly fair to seem to make the democratic idea responsible for Belsen and Buchenwald, any more than it would be fair to attribute the more demoniac vagaries of the Emperor Frederick II, seven centuries earlier, to the idea of the Holy Roman Empire.[1] Perhaps, too, cruelty is never, in itself, the worst crime or the worst danger; Dante may have been right when he placed Frederick's brute imperial vicar in the river of blood among the tyrants, but Frederick himself in one of the burning tombs of the great heresiarchs.

In this study, at any rate, we are concerned, not with tyranny, but with a heresy: the heresy of popular sovereignty. During the last 150 years that heresy may have been the regular highway to

---

[1] All the same, readers of Kantorowicz's *Frederick the Second* cannot help noting both the shuddering fascination which this Emperor's memory still exerts on a humane German mind, and also the ominous ring of the tribute paid to him as the founder of the University of Naples by anonymous Germans in 1924, in the name of *das geheime Deutschland*.

tyranny, but even now not all tyrants travel by that road. More commonly they travel by the by-road of nationalism which, starting as an offshoot from the democratic highway, can easily forget its origin and take a direction of its own. The Europe which emerged from the Peace of Versailles was a nationalist, but not, strictly speaking, a democratic Europe. Outside Germany and Russia, the dictatorships of Europe and Western Asia between the two world wars, from Lisbon to Ankara, were most often mere reactions against the inefficiency and corruption of parliamentary governments, mere experiments in economic and social reconstruction within the framework of old traditions. Among them all, the only one that might belong to the strict history of democracy was Ataturk's; for he succeeded at least in founding a system of government, explicitly based upon the theory of popular sovereignty, with an executive directly dependent upon an elected assembly, which has proved strong enough to survive his death.

Certainly, Italian Fascism does not properly belong to the history of democracy. Mussolini himself may have learned totalism in the school of a Social Democratic Party; but his denial of the debt was unmistakably genuine. His one claim to originality was that he misled a whole generation of would-be imitators into supposing that his version of the traditional Italian 'politics of the piazza' could be exported to other countries. "One cannot" said Louis Blanc of Lamartine "govern permanently by making speeches from the balcony"; nor can one govern, at any rate outside Italy, by para-military marchings and mass meetings. Behind the screen of its Grand Council, its Youth and its militia, the Fascist Party was politically bankrupt. It had no ideology save national pride, coupled with an infinite faith in 'discipline' as the foundation of a Roman *virtù;* its policies were a hotchpotch of expedients, drawn partly, perhaps, from the old armouries of revolutionary democracy, but partly also, as in the case of the 'corporative State', from the bright ideas of current social-ism. Some of its best legislation, such as the Gentile reforms in education, were regarded by many of its members as mere liberalism, unworthy of an Augustan New Order. The only education that mattered was the para-military one of the Party Youth movement; any schooling must be suspect which might develop intellectual tastes and abilities too refined for the enthusiasm of that movement, or too advanced for the economic opportunities available to Italians in a world of unemployment and dislocated trade.

In short, the history of Europe between the wars cannot be written merely in terms of democracy, nor even merely in terms of politics. Those years did not simply mark the culmination of the democratic idea of the State, the logical catastrophe of the one hundred and fifty clearly marked years 1789–1939. The truth is more complicated than that. This century and a half had been the period also of the rise and decline of what is roughly known as the capitalist system; and the history of Europe between the wars can, perhaps, be most justly written as the portrait of a society left derelict by the wreck of that system. True, the democratic idea, in its nationalist form, had its part in hastening the wreck and intensifying the dereliction. Though, as we have said, most of the members of the new family of nations, created by the Peace of Versailles, cannot, either in their constitutions or their operations, be safely classed as pure democracies, they were nationalist States, and such States cannot deny their own revolutionary title deeds. They existed, so the argument had run, because their people were entitled to sovereignty. If their governors could not find a way to be democratic nationalists, they were bound to try to assert themselves as economic nationalists. For the corporate franchises and the international dealings of world capitalism are the most irritating possible challenge to the claim of a sovereign people to sole power within its own territory. An economic democracy must be a closed system; hence Marx's thesis that it could be established only in a World State as the result of an international revolution. But, apart from this conflict, capitalism, as both Marx and Mill foresaw, could, at best, be only a phase in world history; it must by its very nature, either collapse into, or slow down towards, another form of economic society, a 'social democracy' or a 'stationary state'. The tragedy of the years between the wars was that this decline of capitalism coincided in Europe with the culmination of nationalism, and the meeting of the two currents drove the ship of European civilization on the rocks.

Thus, to vary the metaphor, the best diagnosis of the convulsions of Europe between the wars is that they were the result of economic shock, operating on a constitution undermined by the peculiar religious mania of nationalism. The curious thing is that neither branch of that diagnosis seems to have been foreseen by any of the younger men in England who were concerned in any degree with the formulation of Allied war aims between 1914 and 1918. This confession ought to be made by one who was himself in those days a Foreign Office clerk. Mr Balfour might record in a State paper his misgivings about the dissolution of the Austrian Empire; Sir Edward Grey might receive M. Supilo, the Croat leader, with polite reserve; Sir Arthur Nicolson might wish to hold aloof from Balkan feuds; Sir Eyre Crowe might resist the substitution of any semi-parliamentary Council of Nations for the more flexible diplomatic methods of the old Concert of Europe – but to their juniors these hesitations seemed an echo of what they had been taught to regard as the hopeless desire of English conservatives in 1859, including the Queen and the Prince Consort, to uphold the sanctity of the Treaties of 1815 against Italian nationalism and Louis Napoleon. The views of this younger generation were almost accurately represented by a book[1] published in 1915, intended primarily for the instruction of working

---

[1] *The War and Democracy*. Macmillan, 1915, by R. W. Seton Watson and others.

men, which set on its title page a quotation from Mazzini in 1832:

To remake the map of Europe and to re-arrange the peoples in accordance with the special mission assigned to each of them by geographical, ethnical and historical conditions – this is the first essential step for all.

They would, doubtless, have pleaded that, in all this, they were not advocating a policy, but were only recognizing facts; certainly, by the time the Peace Conference met in 1919, there was little left for them to do but to recognize the facts; but there was a light-hearted welcome in their recognition of them, which was significant of much that was to come.

2

The usual criticism of British governments in the 1930's is that, failing to foresee German aggression, they neglected either to make clear their determination to resist it or to arm themselves to make that determination effective.

At the bar of personal responsibility, few who held any office in any of the Cabinets concerned are likely to contest the substantial justice of that charge. But at the remoter bar of history one may doubt whether it will be held to account sufficiently for the curious half-heartedness which afflicted Cabinets, parliaments and people during those years.

For, at that bar, the legends which have been embroidered on the main charge will be difficult to prove. It is not, apparently, true that the catastrophe was unforeseen. There was probably no time, at least from 1934 onwards, when the prospect of war with Germany was not the haunting background of all British policy. Indeed, that pre-occupation largely accounted for the spectacular failure of British policy when faced unexpectedly in 1935 with Italian aggression in Abyssinia. Nor, on the paper record, is it true that the people were not warned of the danger by their official leaders; it will be easy for the future historian to compile from Hansard and the press a whole anthology of warnings, in Parliament and in the constituencies. It is not even true that the governments concerned had no declared policy of re-armament, from the White Paper of 1934 onwards. What is true is that 'haunting background' was an only too accurate description of the British official attitude of mind; that the warnings were muffled and misunderstood;[1] and that re-armament, at least of the land forces,[2] was so technically fumbled as to argue inattention.

There were many reasons for this vagueness; but somewhere near the heart of it was surely a confusion of tongues. The language of war aims and peace settlement in 1917–19 had been that of a family of democratic nations, and of a league of such nations for the prevention of war and the remedy of grievances,[3] each with an equal voice in the public deliberations of the League and a proportionate share in the burdens of a 'pooled security'. In that language the chief danger to peace was expressed as the danger of an armed and undemocratic Germany. Throughout the 1920's the danger was therefore supposed to lie in the revival of the German General Staff, under the quiet camouflaging hand of von

---

[1] The historian will find an odd example of misunderstanding in the impression produced by Mr Churchill's speech of November 7, 1933, on the text: "You cannot be the saviours of Europe on a limited liability". At the time, Professor Toynbee interpreted this speech as advocating a withdrawal from the entanglements of European security. (*Survey of International Affairs,* 1933, pp. 160 and 170.)

[2] Including the air forces as an essential arm of an overseas expeditionary force. Otherwise, much of the early criticism, in 1934–6, of the inadequacy of British re-armament plans in the air, in relation to German air re-armament, was probably misconceived and had two unfortunate results. It tended to create a false sense of insecurity at home at a period when German air power was still negligible; and it tended, much more, to divert parliamentary attention in 1936, and later, from the overriding problem of army re-organization and re-equipment.

[3] Article XIX of the covenant was at least as seriously intended, when it was drafted, as Article X; and it is often forgotten that Sir Samuel Hoare, in his speech at Geneva in September 1935, coupled that principle with the better advertised principle of 'resistance to unprovoked aggression', in describing the policy of the League.

Seekt, and in the accession of Hindenburg to the Presidency. For those who spoke this language, protection against the danger must be sought in a 'global security' agreement, such as the Protocol of 1924, or the narrower Locarno Treaties of 1926, relying primarily on 'economic sanctions', coupled with a measured reduction of armaments and an early liquidation of the temporary clauses of the Peace Treaties, for the benefit of a genuinely democratic Germany.

But, even in the 1920's and still more in the succeeding decade, this language could not be the language of facts. Once more it had become evident, as it had been evident to Canning a century before, that "the general acquisition of free institutions is not necessarily a security for general peace". The facts were: a United States, aloof or hostile, blocking the effective use of economic sanctions, and a Europe too economically insecure to risk their partial imposition; a group of hardening national States, democratic in origin but dictatorial in government, increasingly intolerant of their national minorities, and bringing all their public negotiations for a permanent international settlement to a degree of deadlock almost unknown to the 'old diplomacy'; and a German danger no longer embodied primarily in a General Staff or Army, but in an insurgent people, claiming the 'right to work' in a territory sufficiently extended, and a State effectively socialized, for that purpose. For Britain, the language appropriate to these facts was that of a return to her traditional policy, not indeed of isolation, but of a free hand to co-operate with like-minded continental nations in defence of her national interests, including her most ancient interest of preventing the domination of Europe by any single Power or group of Powers. The League, created in the name of law, was losing its moral authority, much as both the Holy Alliance and the Quadruple Alliance had lost it a century before; there remained only the possibility of constituting an effective Vigilance Committee against robbery and murder.

From this confusion of tongues proceeded the vagaries of British policy in Europe[1] in the seven fatal years 1929–1936. That period began with a popular revolt, in the General Election of 1929, against Anglo-French co-operation, resulting in the strange spectacle of a Chancellor of the Exchequer receiving the Freedom of the City of London for having insulted a French Finance Minister. It ended in an attempt to constitute a Vigilance Committee at Stresa in the spring of 1935, followed by a hectic attempt to mobilize the League against one member of that Committee in the autumn of the same year. Or, from a slightly different point of view, it may be said to have ended in a public opinion ready, that autumn, to impose sanctions on a Fascist Italy in defence of Abyssinia, but unwilling, six months later, to resist in any way the occupation of the Rhineland by a still nominally 'democratic' Germany, in defence of international law.

This idea of a nominally democratic Germany played a special, though now almost forgotten, part in the confusion of tongues. Another moral frequently drawn, since the last war, from the failure of the League of Nations is that its principle of non-interference in the internal affairs of States was outmoded – that Fascism and Nazism should have been recognized, from the outset, as public enemies *per se*, quite apart from their tendencies towards international aggression. The future historian will probably not be disposed to blame the authors of the Covenant for having thus deliberately excluded from its terms any clause which could have authorized a revival of the ambitions of the Holy Alliance; but, even more, he will have to point out that, if the British people had been willing to intervene in the internal affairs of any State in the period 1933–6, it is highly doubtful whether they would have chosen Nazi Germany for the experiment.

---

[1] A consideration of Far Eastern policy would lead us too far from our main theme.

German political language, ever since 1919, had had strange affinities with that of the Independent Labour Party in England. Weber was no socialist, yet, as we have seen,[1] the word 'socialization' rose easily to his lips. Still less was Count Brockdorf-Rantzau a socialist, yet in June 1919 at Versailles, he could formulate the future policy of Germany as

an inexorable declaration of war against capitalism and imperialism, as they are inscribed in the draft peace treaty.

In 1935, a German exile warned Europe that

whoever believes that the word 'socialism' in Germany carries the milder meaning of mere honourable social-mindedness . . . will do well to correct his error. He should acquaint himself with the journals and pamphlets of German Youth, read, as they are, by millions . . . with their talk of 'profit motive' and 'money bags' . . . . In the aims of National Socialism, the emphasis is on the second half of the title; the first is taken for granted.[2]

The cruelties of German anti-Semitism were not enough, until too late, to rouse Englishmen against a popular movement whose speech seemed to echo the speech of perhaps one Englishman in every three during the General Election of 1931, when the common interpretation of the financial crisis was that it was a 'bankers' ramp'. On the contrary, Englishmen were more likely to favour such a movement when it turned against Austrian leaders, no less dictatorial, who had so ruthlessly suppressed, in Vienna, a rising, not of Jews, but of socialist working men.

3

This chapter does not, of course, pretend to be a sufficient summary, either of the state of Europe or of British policy between the wars. Its intention is simply to suggest that the attempt to evolve in Europe an international system of law enforcement and

---

[1] Supra p. 85.
[2] *Not, Kampf, Ziel.* Reinhold Schairer. Societass-Verlag Frankfurt, 1935.

lawful change out of a community of professedly democratic
nations was foredoomed to failure, because, of all forms of State
sovereignty, democracy is the most absolute, the least likely to
subordinate itself to any general overriding law, the least capable
of compromise or of adaption to changing circumstances. It is
doubtful whether such a system would have been compatible
with international capitalism and world trade, as they flourished
in the nineteenth century; it was certainly incompatible with them
as they began to wither in the twentieth. When Woodrow Wilson
spoke of "making the world safe for democracy", he no doubt
believed himself to be merely extending a principle once enunciated by Palmerston:

Constitutional States I consider to be the natural allies of this country. . . .
No English ministry will perform its duty if it be inattentive to the
interests of such States.

But, in fact, he was declaring an exactly opposite principle; he was
committing the old Liberal blunder of mistaking the dogma of
popular sovereignty for the practice of parliamentary government by popular consent.

The French Revolution destroyed for ever that rational, if
restricted, idea of a System of Europe based upon a Balance of
Power, which had dominated the mind of English statesmen in the
eighteenth century and had, within its limits, been almost
realized by Continental statesmen in the thirty years of peace
from 1763 to 1792.[1] It is conceivable that, if the French Revolu-

---

[1] Within its limits, and therefore excluding America and Turkey. Even so,
it was of course, not a complete peace; but, between Frederick the Great's
last victory at Cassel in October 1762 and the cannonade of Valmy in August
1792, no battle was fought on the old soil of Europe; no siege was laid except
at the extreme south-western and north-eastern corners of the Continent, at
Gibraltar and Minorca in 1779–82 and on the Finnish frontier in 1787–90;
and no army moved, except in the bloodless parade of the First Partition of
Poland, in the short stalemate campaign of 1778 in Bohemia, and in the
Prussian demonstration against Holland in 1787. This seems, on the whole,

tion had gone no further than the American one, the System might have adapted itself, without the idealist interruption of the Holy Alliance, to parliamentary government and the industrial revolution, and might have grown gradually to embrace the Debateable Lands of Europe on the Black Sea and the Aegean. It might have established a genuinely liberal internationalism, sounder than the predominantly conservative Concert of Europe which uneasily maintained the Balance of Power for forty years after 1870. It would have been, by Utopian standards, a cynical system, applying to international affairs the principle of "the greatest good of the greatest number", as stated in passing by Beccaria and developed by Bentham into the cold doctrine of Utility. But, after all, it was on that principle that so good a liberal as John Morley justified, in retrospect, the partitioning of Poland, on the ground that Prussia's desire for coherent territories and Russia's desire to unify Orthodox populations under her rule, were of greater and more permanent utility to European society than the nuisance value of Poland's right to a chaotic independence. Such a system would not have created a World State or a Great Society; but it might have made the world safe for the enjoyment and exercise of civic liberties, and even for the development of the 'Welfare State'.

Anyone can play the game of historical might-have-beens. But the game has its legitimate uses. It is not a question of imagining which might have happened if mankind could only have stood still; it is a question of locating the point at which mankind had to make a particular choice and took a particular turning on its journey. It may seem absurd to suggest that, at the end of the eighteenth century, Europe had moved closer to the idea of a Law of Nations than it ever did in the nineteenth and twentieth;

---

a better example of eighteenth century peace than the earlier period between 1713 and 1738, presided over by Walpole and Fleury, but both periods are interesting signs of the growth of a System.

but, on the whole, it is true that, at that point, a Europe in which law had been constantly broken chose to adopt, and in course of time to teach the world, a doctrine of State sovereignty which led inevitably to the positive assertion of international lawlessness as the essential principle of all government. A mere breaker of the law, like Frederick the Great, may always be saved; but there is no salvation for the deniers of law.

In our days the denial of law has become the more general because, by reaction against the lawlessness of democratic nationalism, the conception of international law has tended to harden until it has almost ceased to offer any practical guide to the conduct of international relations. Recently an American diplomatist, criticizing the moralistic-legalistic tradition of American foreign policy, has seemed to see no way of reconciling a reasonable diplomacy of adjustment between competing national interests with the existence of any valid law of nations.[1] This false dilemma indicates how far we have travelled from the eighteenth century. There can be no political system without law; there can be no useful diplomacy of adjustment if the settlement of today may be freely challenged tomorrow. But nowadays, instead of law thus conceived as a code of conduct, worked out progressively by the partners in a political system, as the normal standard to which they will expect each other to conform, we have been invited by jurists to acknowledge something like an absolute 'natural' law, pre-existing and pre-determining all permissible political systems.

And not by jurists alone. The drafters of the Covenant of the League of Nations in Paris in 1919 resisted the desire of jurists like Léon Bourgeois to base the proceedings of the League primarily upon the judgments of a World Court, but they fell easy victims to Woodrow Wilson's choice of the title 'Covenant', with all its seventeenth-century implications of a claim to formu-

---

[1] George F. Kennan, *American Diplomacy 1900–1950*, Secker and Warburg 1952.

late absolute truth as a guide to political action. Conformably
to this name, the popular ideal of the League of Nations came to
be the Utopian one of a universal enforcement of law, authorita-
tively, if not judicially, pronounced. In the light of that ideal,
economic sanctions by all nations, not military action by some,
should be the sole means of enforcement; attempts to conciliate
had an air of collusion and military agreements to coerce possible
aggressors an air of brigandage. Secret diplomacy and the balance
of power must go, as relics of an old pre-democratic age of
unenlightenment. Thus international discomforts were left to
grow into world disputes, and then the Utopians found themselves morally bound, but physically powerless, to protect a mere
status quo.

Caught thus between the two absolutes of natural law and
popular sovereignty, Western Europe and America have almost
lost the modest sense of what Gladstone, in an attack on Palmerston's foreign policy, called "the moral supports which the general
and fixed convictions of mankind afford" and, losing that, they
have lost any practical standard by which they can distinguish
the changes necessary to the preservation of a peaceful international
system from breaches of its rules which would undermine its
existence.

What then? Have we, in the mid-twentieth century, no longer
any other choice than between a Socialist World State on the
Russian model, and a restless community of disillusioned parliamentary 'democracies', still vainly endeavouring to combine the
absolute dogmas of popular sovereignty with the modest compromises of government by free discussion and popular consent?
If we reject the first, must we live indefinitely in the second,
perpetually on the defensive, confessing no coherent political
faith and guided by no clear sense of direction? If we are to
answer that question, we must examine the idea of government
by popular consent as we have already tried to examine the rival

idea of government by popular sovereignty. But let us understand at the outset that, in doing so, we shall not be contrasting an ancient and established idea of government with a new and revolutionary one. The idea of government by popular consent has, indeed, much the longer history, but also much the more incoherent one. It has been, always but obscurely, based upon a philosophy of dualism, as its rival has been, much more explicitly, based upon a philosophy of totalism; and to formulate a philosophy of dualism, with all that it implies, as the explicit foundation of a modern system of government is, today, a more revolutionary undertaking than to accept the now almost established system of total democracy.

III

The idea of government by consent,
Pre-Christian and Christian

The first two sections of this study have led to the conclusion that the world needs a philosophy of Dualism which can be set effectively against the democratic philosophy of Totalism. The argument of this third section is that, in fact, the whole history of civilization, from the primitive village communities of the East to the barbarian conquest of Western Europe in the fifth century, has consisted in the working out of a Dualist idea which is inseparable from the idea of the Moral State. To these twin ideas Christianity gave a new coherence and a new power to express themselves on the scale of the region-State. But, in speaking of Christianity, a distinction has to be drawn between the original Christian philosophy of 'Church' and 'world' and the very different, and much less coherent, philosophy of 'Christendom' which emerged after the Christianization of the Empire and the fall of Rome. This distinction is crucial to an understanding of political development in mediaeval and modern Europe, and an attempt is made to reconstruct the original thought of the early Church and to define the nature of the revolution which it underwent in the fifth century, principally under the influence of Augustine.

CHAPTER 9

The moral state

Dualism of law and ethics in the history of civilization – Meaning of history – Meaning of law – The village community and the State: early empires, Palestine, Mediterranean city states, Roman empire and Germanic invaders – The dualism of Christianity: *sacrum* and *regnum;* the idea of the Covenant.

I

The dualism which we have to define is the one which is written large in the history of civilized man: the dualism between State law and human ethics. It can, therefore, best be defined in historical terms, in terms of man's actual experience and of the interpretations which, at various stages in his history, he has put upon his experience.

Man's most consistent effort throughout his history has been to find a way of living at peace with his neighbours on the basis of compulsory rules generally acceptable to their reason and conscience and compatible with their common sense of individual freedom. But, in this effort of civil-ization, he has always recognized reason, conscience and the sense of freedom as the primary authorities which should govern personal conduct; the compulsory rules which he has devised for general enforcement upon himself and his neighbours have never been more than a selection from the vast repertory of human duty and aspiration. Moreover, he has always had to recognize that the very fact of selecting them for general enforcement inevitably changes their character, usually for the worse. The most obvious characteristic of State law is a certain moral dilemma. Those who wield the powers of the State do so in the name of duty; yet they are precluded, to the extent of their political functions, from regulating their conduct wholly by the highest standards of duty inculcated by the greatest moral teachers of mankind. Their family loyalty must fall short of the precepts of Confucius; they must act where the Buddha counselled abstention from action; they must judge where Christ commanded them to forgive. The law of the State cannot coincide with the law of love which binds the individual. In the selection of moral rules for enforcement, and in the decision to pay the necessary moral price for that selection, lies the whole science of jurisprudence; that science is based on the axiom that personal ethics cannot be directly translated into civilized law.

2

Here, at the outset of our argument, we must pause to explain our language. Obviously, 'ethics', in the sense in which we are using the word, must be understood to include, not only a man's standards of action, but also his ideas of the universe in relation to himself. It includes both his moral philosophy and his religion. What is not so obvious is our use of the sweeping words 'always' and 'never'. These words are true only subject to two reservations.

First, they are true only in the context of History. History is the record of

the last five or six thousand years within which mankind, after having been human for at least six hundred thousand years before that, attained the modest level of social and moral achievement that we call civilization.[1]

And, since all men have not, even now, attained that level, History is confined to those who have. It knows nothing of the 'primitive' societies, studied and described by anthropologists, whose distinguishing characteristic seems to be the total identification of law with ethics. Whether this was also the character-

---

[1] Arnold J. Toynbee. *Civilization on Trial.* Oxford University Press. The present writer would hesitate to commit himself to the estimate of 600,000 years as the age of *homo sapiens;* but that point is unimportant.

istic of the pre-historical societies from which what we call civilization originally emerged, we do not know; we know only that, if so, it did emerge from them and shed their peculiarities. We can infer, perhaps, that the 'primitive' societies of the anthropologist are old societies which, failing to advance beyond that stage, have allowed their 'total' rule of life to harden into a mould so fixed as to preclude further development, because it leaves their members too little scope for individual differentiation. If there is any meaning in the words 'barbarism' and 'savagery', this is their meaning.

And our second reservation (which may cast a doubt on the chronological primitiveness of all 'primitive' man) must be that, even within History as we have defined it, societies already civilized have not seldom shown a tendency to relapse into barbarism of this kind. These relapses are distinguishable from the much more frequent lapses of all civilized societies into the mere tyranny of personal rule. Personal tyranny may be arbitrary, but it is seldom 'total'. Indeed, under a Justinian or a Napoleon mankind has often made its greatest advances in jurisprudence. The relapses, properly so called, have, in historic times, been rare and relatively brief. They have been both intolerable and debilitating, and have ended either in revolt or in conquest – in revolt, because even rudimentarily civilized man does not easily forget freedoms once enjoyed; in conquest, because civilization does not even begin to grow in the isolation which has, until quite recent times, protected the barbarisms of Central Africa or the Pacific islands.[1]

---

[1] It is not easy to give examples of this tendency to relapse, without involving oneself in lengthy historical argument. It may suffice to say that the tendency seems to have been specially characterisic of small closely-knit States, in particular City States like fourth century Athens. Aristotle has left a recognizable picture of *Gleichschaltung* in his own day: "The last form of democracy, that in which all share alike, is one which cannot be borne by all states and will not last long unless well-regulated by laws and customs". The citizen body must be diluted by aliens or semi-aliens; "fresh tribes and brotherhoods must be established; the private rites of families must be re-

Modern totalism is the latest, and the worst, of these relapses. Whether, in the form of an almost continental communist State, isolated behind an Iron Curtain, it, too, will prove to be short-lived, is the grand question of contemporary politics.

3

Further our language needs one more important explanation. When we speak of law, we should make it clear that we are using that word seriously. In an earlier chapter, we have discussed the growing modern fashion of social-ism, the attempt to escape from the study of government into the study of some vaguer entity called 'society'. The argument upon which we have now embarked would be meaningless if we did not insist on the reality and distinctness of the ideas of Law, and of the State as the author and enforcer of Law.

The oldest vice of political thought has been a weak craving for analogies. The two most popular analogies have been with the human body and with physical order in the universe. Modern science has given a new twist to each of these myths; to the myth of the 'body politic', an evolutionary twist; to the myth of a 'political system', a twist away from the 'degree, priority and place' of sun and planets towards the miniature constellations of sub-atomic physics. This latest analogy has proved especially seductive, because it seems to get rid of the uncomfortable con-

---

stricted and converted into public ones; in short, every contrivance must be adopted which will mingle the citizens with one another and get rid of old connections". (*Politics* VI 4.) It must be remembered that Greek political philosophy had itself strong totalist tendencies, modified only by a tradition of 'go as you please' in social manners. Aristotle, no less than Plato believed that "the citizen should be moulded to suit the form of government under which he lives", that "education should be one and the same for all" and that no "citizen belongs to himself, for all belong to the State". Christianity introduced a different philosophy and, though analogous tendencies may be traced in fourteenth century Florence, in the Nürnberg of the Renaissance and, still more, in Calvin's Geneva and in Puritan New England, they are not so clear, and are complicated by other factors.

trast between political and natural law. It tends to reduce both to a mere law of averages: a normal 'pattern of behaviour' which the physicist can discern in his electrons and the vital statistician or the psychologist in the human citizen.

The fallacy of all such pretty pictures is the assumption that a human society is either a self-evident entity like the human body, or has been ascertained to be an entity by investigations of its structure as thorough as those of the astronomer and the physicist. That assumption is the charter of what are now called the 'social sciences'; and it is false. A society is simply a number of human beings living in a certain degree of geographical contiguity. Every science which is concerned with the study of individual man is a social science, in the sense that man is a gregarious animal; but in any other sense there is only one social science. What the 'social' psychologist or biologist, or the professor of 'social' medicine, really means by his title is that, especially under modern conditions of life, there are certain aspects of his science which are of immediate concern to governments. In other words, the only social science is political science.

Political science is the study of human beings living in a particular kind of association, called a State, where they regulate some part of their conduct in obedience to rules enforced upon them by persons selected for that purpose, in accordance with procedures laid down beforehand. This identification of political action with the regulated exercise of force is an unpopular fact, because, when divorced from the corresponding fact that such force can be tolerably exercised only by consent of the body of citizens, it has been made the starting point of a dozen rash philosophies about the origin and purpose of political authority. But it is a fact. The distinguishing mark of the citizen is that, as such, he is the object of regulated compulsion to social behaviour, in contrast to the members of any other community who, as such, are liable only to expulsion for unsocial behaviour. And the distinguishing mark of the free citizen is, not only that he accepts that compulsion, but that, in greater or less degree, he shares in its exercise. This compulsion is the only purely social fact. All other social activities become social because they are already the activities of individuals, singly or by twos and threes. Law alone is a new creation in society; and the State, in which it is created, is the only society which is something more than the aggregate of the actions and interactions of its individual members.

To assert this is not, of course, to deny that there are other forms of association which influence, and, indeed, regulate, their members in particular ways, or that these influences and regulations – let us say industrial fatigue or agreed trade practices – may be scientifically studied without direct reference to State policy. Nor is it to deny that, in the words of a modernist teacher of law:

> There is a vast amount of authentic legal tissue which lies outside the jurisdiction of the Courts and beyond the ken of legislative assemblies and government departments. To ignore it is to shut one's eyes to much that is highly significant and interesting in the evolution of law.[1]

But the significance of such tissue is that it *is* evolving towards law. The oldest of the 'Social sciences', economics, though largely concerned with non-political forms of association, was born and throve in England as an effort to teach wisdom to statesmen. Since English economists won their political point in free trade, their successors have tended to lose themselves in social surveys which they cannot focus in terms of State action. A similar doom of ineffectiveness seems to haunt the new 'science' of town and country planning; it has remained a social aspiration because its exponents have failed to set it in the framework of a political doctrine. In England, the one major piece of legislation which they have inspired is so confused in machinery and purpose that it has proved largely unworkable.

---

[1] W. A. Robson. *Civilisation and the growth of Law.* Macmillan, 1935.

The same doom haunts also the recent fashion of 'social' history, with its somewhat impish handmaid anthropology. The historian must, indeed, humble himself always to remember the humanist's confession of faith: that manhood and womanhood are more wonderful than citizenship, and that men are greater than their institutions. But he must not turn truth into nonsense by supposing that they are more social than their institutions. History is focus, and the focus of a society is in the constitution and commands of its sovereign. By man's political fruits alone can his social character be historically judged.

4

It is, then, in these terms that we have to study the saving dualism of the civilizing process, which has produced the State systems of Europe and America. In its earliest stages, this dualism seems to have taken the crude form of a divorce between the State itself and the moral law. At this stage, moreover, the State included organized religion; in the close alliance between king and priest which we can discern in the earliest empires – in Egypt, Babylon and Persia, for instance – it is doubtful whether priesthood represented the moral order any more than kingship. But from these beginnings, the history of civilized man is the history of the creation of the Moral State – still a dualism, but a dualism, not of divorce, but of marriage. That may be said to be man's one historical achievement; or rather, it is man's one continuous adventure, whose end is still to be achieved. Only along that line is the thread of his history unbroken. It runs, as far back as we can clearly trace it, from Jerusalem to Athens across the catastrophe of the sixth century B.C.; it runs from Rome to Aachen and Winchester across the Dark Ages of our own era.

From the dawn of history in the deltas of the Nile, the Euphrates and the Indus, the village community, developing here and there into city communities, was the unit of the moral law, popularly defined and popularly enforced. It remained so as successive fighting empires engulfed it, levying tribute, exacting service, dictating forms of State worship, taking over such parts of the moral law as seemed essential to developing commerce and to the exercise of imperial power, but leaving its life otherwise untouched and unimitated. Its rudimentary moral integrity was one of tradition and environment, rooted in the conditions of an agricultural economy and incapable of direct transplantation to the wider environment of the State. Even in the small seed-plot of Palestine, where, so far as we know, the experiment of the Moral State first assumed a recognizable form, the transplantation failed.

But the Palestine experiment was, in at least two ways, a new departure. The Jewish State grew, not directly out of one of the immemorial agricultural village economies of the great river valleys – nor out of any city which emerged from them on the intersection of caravan routes – but out of a migrant community which, in the wanderings and temporary settlements of at least 500 years, had developed a tribal organization, requiring some form of central leadership, and did not finally settle down to an agricultural life until a comparatively late stage in its history, in a newly conquered country. Consequently, this community deliberately adopted, as a necessary means of unity, a moral law and a religion which had not grown naturally out of its own tradition, or out of the changing environments through which it had passed, and was in sharp contrast with the village traditions of the country it conquered. The result was that its moral law – the *Law of the Covenant* – was, from the first, associated with a central seat of authority, representing the unity of the people; and the failure of the experiment lay in the failure of this central authority continuously to preserve its moral law and to assert it against the indigenous idolatries of the countryside. Such, at least, was the memory which this people retained of their origins and their history.

After the Jewish failure, the adventure of the Moral State passed to European soil, where it had much the same mixed origins in the migratory conquests and settlements of the 2,000 years or so between (say) 1000. B.C. and A.D. 1000. First, in Greece, the City State was created by unions of village communities, but, in the mind of later generations, the memory of these unions was mixed with other memories, such as one might expect from a migratory history, of patriarchal kings ruling, sometimes over compact family units, sometimes over "colonies of the family . . . living dispersedly".[1] In spite, however, of these traces of chieftainship and clan organization, the Greek experiment was in the nature of a direct translation of village into city, and went no further. In the process, arrested at that point, the village community lost much of its own moral integrity, but failed to find a new one. That failure generated some of the most powerful political thinking in human history, as the Jewish failure had generated some of the most powerful religious thinking; but for that, both experiments might be written off as the Neanderthal men of political evolution. Republican Rome failed too, but left its own peculiar legacy, not only of legal thought, but also of legal practice. The age of empires returned, until the old adventure began afresh in the manorial or 'folk-moot' villages of Germanic invaders.

At this point something happened. In the course of centuries, this new experiment was pushed much farther than the old, into the creation of the Region-State.[2] Throughout Europe it grew into federations, into local parliamentary institutions, until, where the process was not cut short, folk custom grew into the common law of a nation and the delegates of local communities, who came

---

[1] Aristotle. *Politics* I. 2.
[2] Usually distinguished as the Nation-State, but the idea of nationality was a later growth, however much nineteenth century writers may have taken it for granted. The neutral geographical term seems the best.

to grant subsidies to the central administration, became the representative governors of the realm.

True, the process was so generally cut short in continental Europe that its complete pattern can, perhaps, be traced only in England. It required for its success the co-operation of strong centralizing monarchies with equally strong centres of local autonomy; where either side of the balance failed, representative institutions were either extinguished, or hardened into mere privileged 'Estates'. But the idea of popular assent, as an essential element in moral government, persisted under even the most unlikely forms. Thus, in 1652, it could be claimed for the lawyer's Parlement of Paris that

it is a fundamental law of the kingdom that nothing can be imposed on the king's subjects, and that no new office can be created, save by the consent of the Parlement which represents the general judgment (*aveu*) of the whole people.[1]

It can hardly be doubted that, in these latest thousand years of human history, the old adventure of the Moral State, which had so often ended in a blind alley, did show a new vitality, a new capacity for expressing moral integrity on the scale of full State government, and also a new power of recovery after temporary failures. Nor can it be seriously doubted that it derived this power from the new sanction given by Christianity to the pre-Christian idea of the Moral State.

5

The newness of this sanction is apt to be overlooked, partly because it has become so familiar, partly because so many of its manifestations in politics have been so questionable. The part played by the Christian Church in this latest stage of the adventure of the Moral State has been exasperatingly ambiguous; indeed,

---

[1] *De la Nature et qualité du Parlement de Paris*, 1652. Quoted from Hanotaux. *La France en 1614*, Nelson 1913.

the Christian, even more than the free-thinker, may be tempted to call it treacherous. We shall have something to say about that unhappy story in a later chapter. But, athwart all the strife of tongues and ambitions which has disfigured the history of Christendom, the central teaching of the Church continued, from first to last, to insist on two essential and contrasted propositions, one as old as Judaism, but the other startlingly new: on the one hand, the single divine origin of all social obligation and of all social authority in a "righteous God who loveth righteousness"; on the other hand, the dualism, within one *Respublica Christiana,* between two distinct authorities, the *Sacrum* and the *Regnum,* the Church and the State. It is small wonder that even wise men should have stumbled in striking a stable balance in this dualism, or in reconciling the second proposition with the first.

There was only one way of reconciliation, one inherent in all Christian teaching and practice, but only slowly apprehended in its application to the philosophy of the State. If the one Christian Commonwealth does not derive its unity from a single mundane authority, it must derive it from the consensus of all its citizens. If the one righteous God has made no single authority responsible for interpreting His whole social law of righteousness, responsibility must rest with the individual members of society, at least to the extent of their choice between interpreters. And, if they are to discharge their responsibility intelligently, it follows that the law must have been, in some sense, delivered to them and accepted by them. That delivery and that acceptance had been postulated of the Jewish citizen by the old doctrine of the Covenant; it could, with much greater show of reason, be postulated of the baptized Christian, especially in the early days of European Christendom when the law had been so recently delivered by a missionary Church and popular acceptance so recently attested by conversion from heathenism. If it was God's way thus to submit His law to popular consent, could any earthly ruler claim to exercise more arbitrarily the power delegated to him by God?

The emergence of this idea that truth is not an esoteric secret, but is publicly revealed, is, perhaps, the greatest landmark in the history of human thought. The historian dates it from its classic expression, at least 2,500 years ago, in the declaration: "The word is very nigh unto thee, in thy mouth and in thy heart, that thou mayest do it."[1] The modern rationalist, discarding history for anthropology, ignores it and supposes that "it is only during the past three centuries" of scientific enlightenment that man has begun to desert the belief

that both human existence and the physical universe were alike subject to unpredictable and inscrutable interferences on the part of magical and supernatural forces.[2]

But we are writing in terms of history, and, as a matter of historical fact, it was across this bridge of reconciliation that the transplantation of the moral law from the local to the regional community was successfully carried out. If the primitive village community was the original unit of the moral law, it was the unit also of superstition and lynch law, from the vegetation magic and human sacrifices of the Levant to the *lex talionis* and the blood feuds of Germanic tribes. The moral law of the village could not be directly transplanted because its roots were entangled with these other roots;[3] it could be transplanted only by being reformulated and redelivered by a more than popular authority. The Moral State begins always in such a new delivery and acceptance of the Law. The original Lawgiver is a distinct key-figure in all early tradition: Moses, Solon, the decemvirs of the Twelve Tables and, more fictitiously, the 'laws of Edward the Confessor'. Such

---

[1] Deuteronomy 30. 14.

[2] W. A. Robson. *Op. cit.*

[3] This point is illustrated by the 'laws of Hamurabbi', the Babylonian code which combined a quite advanced system of commercial law with a wholly primitive code of criminal penalties.

a 'covenant' is especially essential in the creation of a region-state, for no code of personal relations between citizens can be centrally enforced in such a state during the formative stages of its development unless it represents the moral sense of local communities who will co-operate in its enforcement. For that purpose, the force of law must depend on something more rational than what Aristotle called "a habit of obedience which can be given only by time".[1] In spite of all earlier experiments, it is fair to say that these twin ideas of lawgiving and covenant remained ideas until they were materialized in the society of Christendom: until the centralizing lawgiver became a consecrated king, and the village or borough community a Christian congregation.

But if we are to trace the history of the Christian Moral State from these rudimentary beginnings, we must, for the moment, desert history and consider more philosophically the basic view of human nature on which the dualism of Christendom was originally founded. For if men are to be governed by their own consent, they must be offered a government which proceeds on intelligible principles towards definable purposes. And these principles and purposes must be religious in the sense that they must be based upon a coherent view of what man is, of what constitutes for him a 'good life', and of the means by which it can be obtained. Of such, as we have seen, are the principles and purposes of communism, even when it proclaims the abolition of God; of such were once the principles and purposes of the Christian State even when it denied most flagrantly in its acts the God it professed to worship; of such must be the principles and purposes of any political philosophy which seeks to govern men in the future without repeating the crimes and blunders of the past.

---

[1] Politica II. 8.

CHAPTER 10

The ascent and descent of man

Christian theology – The 'Fall of Man' and the New Biology – The Power State and the Myth of the Cycle – Christian idea of the State as the restorer of a broken law – Revolution in the Christian Church between Constantine and Clovis.

I

We have said that a philosophy of government must be based upon a coherent view of human nature. Now, a base should be broader than the structure it supports. The physician, for example, who believes that physical health is based on mental health, will not be much enlightened by a psychology which can express itself only in physical terms. In the same way, the jurist will not find a secure basis for a philosophy of law in a philosophy of human nature which can express itself only in legal terms – in terms, for instance, of 'natural' rights and enforceable 'natural' duties.

A Christian philosophy of government at least avoids this trick of circular argument. The Christian can express human nature only in terms of its relation to God; and, if God be what the Christian believes Him to be, man can have no rights against Him. Indeed, in any legal sense, man can have no duties to God; for, as we have seen, the essence of legal duty is limitation and definition, but there can be no bounds to the Divine Will, nor to man's function of conformity with it. For the Christian, the Divine Will is the only reality; at the outset of his attempt to understand himself, he must have the courage to forget himself in the presence of the purpose of God.

In the language of Christian belief, the purpose of God is that man who is the image of God shall become partaker also of the nature of God. The means to that end is the knowledge of God. All men are capable of knowing God, but their capacity must be gradually developed. God therefore reveals Himself progressively to men, as they are able to understand Him. As the revelation deepens towards intimacy, it becomes possible to say that God imparts Himself to men as they are able to receive Him, that God dwells in men, and that God's life is manifested in men. To this relationship no man is compelled; and access to it cannot be gained, nor progress in it attested, by observance of a compulsory code. The language appropriate to it is the language of learning and belief, of fatherhood and sonship, and, ultimately, of men changed by full knowledge of God into the likeness of God.

This relationship of men to God has obvious consequences in the relationship of men to each other. In the purpose of God, the community of mankind is a reflection of the communion of its members with God. Its bond is that of a family, growing in the presence of its head, and drawing from him the unconstrained impulse to mutual service. To embody and display this relationship of men to God and of men to each other is the function of the society called the Christian Church. But this society emerged late in the history of mankind and it has performed its function so imperfectly that this description of it may seem a mockery of the facts of Church history. The reason for both the lateness of its appearance and for its gross imperfections is that, at a very early stage in his development, man rejected the direct access to God which he was intended to enjoy. The consequence of that rejection has been, so to speak, a constitutional malady, a corruption of the human appetite and an infirmity of the human will.

2

Here the modern learner of the language of Christian belief encounters the most difficult feature of its grammar: the doctrine of 'the Fall'. Yet it is odd that it should still be such a stumbling-block today. In the second half of the nineteenth century, it is true, the pioneers of the new sciences of biology and anthropology, who have so largely formed the mind of the contemporary world, had their attention so riveted on the idea of the 'Ascent of Man' that to speak of his Fall seemed a blasphemy against scientific truth. But, since then, the climate of scientific opinion has undergone a change. Even the first generation of Darwinians could not deny the hard fact of the contradiction in man's nature pictured long ago by Plato in his image of the charioteer of the middle heavens, one of whose ill-matched pair of horses strains upward to the gods, while the other drags downward to the earth. Indeed, T. H. Huxley was at least half-prepared to regard the evolutionary struggle for existence as itself part of 'the essential evil of the world'. But if, in this sense, these scientists had to admit the existence of 'original sin', they preferred to think of it as the clinging taint of an animal nature, not yet shaken off in man's upward progress. The scientific weakness of this view lay, how-ever, in the fact that the characteristic misbehaviours of historic man were so unlike any 'natural' animal behaviour. The study of history, however far back it might be pushed into the region of comparative anthropology, was, plainly, the study of intellectual or spiritual faculties, which have driven man, in the short space of a few thousand years, through the most violent changes and chances, actions and reactions, aspirations, failures and crimes. To these agitations no theory of mere biological evolution, no talk of mankind taking 'twenty thousand years to transcend the wolf-pack', could have any application whatever. There might be an 'ape and tiger' in man, but man had obviously added to his inherited animalism a good deal which was peculiarly his own.

And so, about the turn of the century, under the influence of the new study of 'social psychology', a new theory of human evolution tended to arise, in which man's most barbaric practices became, not throw-backs to a bad ancestry, but inevitable incidents in his adaptive processes – positive marks, indeed, of his advance towards a larger morality. As thus:

War with its ferocities, cannibalism and slavery are relatively late products in social evolution and incident to man's adjustment to a wider and more complex social environment. . . . It is the struggle and conflict that have been developed within the species in its more complex stages of evolution, that has called forth, sometimes in exaggerated form, the predatory and anti-social tendencies which we see more or less in human society today.[1]

Unfortunately, those who propounded this view neglected to make it clear, even if they were clear about it in their own minds, that 'adjustment to a wider environment' is not a moral duty, while 'predatory and anti-social tendencies' are moral delinquencies. Without that distinction, the words we have quoted would, of course, have served well enough, a short twenty-five years after they were written, for a justification of Hitler's 'new order'; and those who held this view of human progress might have looked on its worst inhumanities, not only with indulgence, but even with the agreeable tremors of a 'larger hope'.

But, in the last few years, the whole scientific discussion has been transformed by biologists who have drawn a new distinction between organic and human evolution – between an 'old evolution' which is 'essentially amoral' and the 'new evolution' of man who is 'a moral animal'. Let us quote again from a much more eminent American authority:[2]

Man is the highest animal. . . . He is also a fundamentally new sort of animal, and one in which, although organic evolution continues on its way, a fundamentally new sort of evolution has also appeared. . . . Organic evolution rejects acquired characters in inheritance and adap-

---

[1] Charles A. Ellwood. *Sociology in its Psychological Aspects*. D. Appleton and Co., 1912.

[2] Dr George Gaylord Simpson. *The Meaning of Evolution*, Yale University Press, 1949.

I

tively orients the essentially random, non-environmental interplay of genetical systems. The new evolution peculiar to man operates directly by the inheritance of acquired characters, of knowledge and learned activities, which arise in, and are continuously a part of, an organismic-environmental system, that of social organization. . . . Purpose and plan are not characteristic of organic evolution and are not a key to its operations. But purpose and plan are characteristic in the new evolution, because man has purposes and he makes plans. . . . Man . . . exercises deliberate choice to a unique degree. . . . It is most improbable that any other animal has more than an inchoate or largely instinctual sense of values, while in man this is normally conscious, orderly, and controlled. . . . Conscious knowledge, purpose, choice and values carry as an inevitable corollary responsibility. . . . Survival, harmony, increase of life, integration of organic or social aggregations, or other such suggested ethical standards, . . . are not really ethical principles. . . . They become ethical principles only if man chooses to make them such. Man cannot evade his responsibility of choice. As his knowledge embraces facts about these characteristics in evolution, they become part of the basis on which his ethical principles should be developed, but they supply no automatic guide to good or bad.

This does not pretend to be Christian doctrine – rather the reverse; but it is not a bad introduction to it. In so momentous a transition as that between an old evolution and a new, what mistakes might not be expected in the exercise of an unaccustomed responsibility of choice? For, as the author of the extracts we have quoted insists, "there is no trend solely in the right direction". True, he still feels it necessary to add that 'man has risen, not fallen'; but, with all respect, those five words have little meaning. A climber who has fallen into a crevasse at the head of a glacier has both risen and fallen. And the Christian doctrine is just that. It is not a doctrine of 'total depravity'. Man has risen from being a creature formed of 'the dust of the ground' to being a 'living soul', but in passing from the old state to the new he has made a wrong choice and taken a wrong turning. Even then, as now, he was capable of 'exercising deliberate choice' -- and he exercised it. Ever since, he has carried within him the consequences both of his rise and of his fall, both of his high calling and of his rejection of it.

3

Perhaps the real stumbling-block is in that word 'rejection'. Is not that to translate into terms of positive action what, at so early a stage, could have been only a negative deafness and ignorance? A staggering and erratic progress, punctuated by a whole series of falls, would be credible enough; but 'a' fall, concentrated into some one signal act of disobedience, looks like an example of the myth-habit which telescopes a course of events into a single catastrophe. Be it so; history and biology alike must be largely written in the language of myth; the 'fall of Rome' is, strictly speaking, a myth, even when preceded by the word 'decline'; by the same token, the 'appearance' of a new sort of evolution is also a myth. On the other hand, as we have already suggested in the first chapter of this essay, the old liberal rationalist habit, which Shaw once satirized in the character of Mazzini Dunn, of thinking that nothing ever *happens* in human history, is a more dangerous, because a more unconscious, form of myth. If we can describe the 'Fall of Man' in terms which will fit the actual tendencies of all human societies, as far back as their historical record goes, we need, perhaps, speculate no further about the original form in which those tendencies were expressed in the unrecorded first stages of the 'new evolution'.

It is not very difficult to do this. From his first appearance in history, man has been the potential ruler of the world, able, alone of all living beings, to grasp the universe by his intellect and to subdue the earth on which he lives to his service. If there is a righteous and active God, His purpose must have been that man, who is strong enough to subdue the earth to his own service, should become wise enough to subdue it to God's service. If so, there could be no road to that particular kind of wisdom save through the knowledge of God; it must be God's purpose that man, perfected in the knowledge of God, shall become the agent and sharer of God's universal rule. But, from the first, man started on his road to power, not empty-headed and empty-minded, but already endowed with enormous capacities. It was not obvious that he needed the knowledge of God; if he turned away from that knowledge, he was apparently wealthy enough to be independent. And, from the first, he chose independence. He preferred to the knowledge of God the knowledge and exploitation of his own power. It was for that purpose that he desired, and attained, the 'knowledge of good and evil'; and he has found in that knowledge, *sought for that purpose,* no sufficient guide to the exercise of his power. Throughout history, *in his pursuit of power,* his politic wisdom, no less than his folly, has turned eventually to his own destruction.

Some may think this a queer description of early historical man, so much engrossed as we know him to have been with the cult of multifarious deities. But his religions, as we also know, were made in the image of his need to dominate nature and of his ambition to dominate his fellow-man. They were, as the anthropologists are so anxious to remind us, never far from self-interested magic, and we have already suggested, in the preceding chapter, that, in their political forms, they had little or nothing to do with the recognition of any moral order.

This will to power, and this measurement of wisdom by its utility as a means to power, have certainly been, as a matter of history, the consistent characteristics of political man, at least ever since he emerged from the village community. It is, of course, perfectly possible to believe that his choice has been right, that there is no God, or at least no God of whose will man could have any certain knowledge, and that man has, therefore, had no alternative to independence. But if there is a God, and if man had any early knowledge of Him, it is not possible to regard his actual

historical record as anything less than a deliberate rejection of
God's will.

4

We have said 'political man'. It is in his attempts to form
governments – to constitute States – that man has most clearly
revealed his character. Many individual men have sought, and
still seek, knowledge for its own sake; but it has been, and still is,
the function of human government to subdue, or to wrest, knowledge to the purposes of power. It is here that the historian and
the theologian alike really part company with the biologist. Even
the new biology of today is impregnated with the fashion of semi-
totalist social-ism which we have described in an earlier chapter.
Seeking in the 'new evolution' a naturalistic ethic proper to
civilized man, the biologist shows little appreciation of the distinction between ethics and law, and little consciousness of the
existence of the State. Consequently, he ignores almost wholly
the historical record of man's political progress. The horror of
that record, measured in terms of human suffering, makes little
impression on him; he may warn men that "there is no trend
solely in the right direction", but he can ignore the evidence that,
over must of the last five or six thousand years, there seems to
have been a trend, if anything, in the wrong direction. Frankly,
can any unprejudiced student discern in history any sign of man's
progress towards a higher evolutionary level of political association, in any of the qualities or modes of action which the best men
value most? The actual record looks much more like the characteristic myth of nearly all, if not all, early human thought – the
myth of the Cycle. Man, as a social or political animal, seems
bound eternally, like nature itself, on a wheel of growth and
decay, destined once, in each cycle, to experience the summer of a
Great Age, only to lose it again in the winter of a new discontent.
At any given point in this periodic rise and fall of civilizations,

not only man, but the gods themselves, seem to be fighting a losing battle, and human virtue may well consist, as our Norse ancestors thought, merely in fighting this battle to the end, counting it honour to be overwhelmed at last with all Valhalla in the encompassing darkness and the roaring of the sea.

True or false, this nightmare did, in fact, represent, up to the last two thousand years or so, man's usual estimate of himself and his destinies. Deliverance from this Wheel of Things was his earliest and most consistent hope, the source of all his 'mystery' religions; and the quality of his hope was the measure of his miseries. It was a hope based on despair of the world; the best conceivable prospect was that individual men might be 'reborn into the eternal' beyond the flux of time. "The worlds come and go, but for them who come to me, Krishna, there is no birth again". Or, if the world was not quite despaired of, hope for it was concentrated in the idea of the appearance of some personal Deliverer, some hero-god, as the introducer of a new Great Age. "Whensoever the law fails and lawlessness uprises, then do I, Krishna, come to bodied birth". As this form of the myth moved westwards, its effect, from Alexander to Diocletian, was to deify despotism, sanctioning its most arbitrary departures from settled law and its proudest claims to universal empire.

True or false, also, the theory of the Fall of Man did, in fact, end this nightmare, because it restored to men the consciousness of their own responsibility. It substituted for the essential moral lawlessness of a nature-myth the idea of a broken law and the possibility of man's return to its obedience. And in that hope Christendom was born.

5

We have said, in the last chapter, that, as a matter of history, the adventure of the Moral State showed a new vitality in its Christian form. It is even more true that, as a matter of ideas, the

Christian conception of the nature of man transfigured man's whole conception of the nature of the State. What had been the incarnation of man's lust for power became the agency for the re-establishment of a broken law. Man had frustrated the purpose of God, but he had not defeated it. The purpose remained unchanged; but the education of man had been set back to a more elementary stage. Having lost his direct access to God by lawlessness, he must be brought back to it by the discipline of law. Having refused to know God as father, he must learn to know Him as master. Law was the restraint of man's lawlessness towards his fellow-man; it was the preliminary remedy for his constitutional malady; but, above all, it was the elementary revelation of God's nature to men who must be schooled in righteousness before they could apprehend love.

'Preliminary' and 'elementary', for, in the Christian conception, the State and its law must have their set limits. Man's way to perfection lies still only through the knowledge of God; he is still bidden to seek direct access to God. Salvation is not by the law, even by God's law; and the limit of State law, even when it reflects most nearly the law of God, is essentially that it must not obstruct God's purpose of perfection.

This distinction (and here we return definitely to the historical record) had been latent in the social life of pagans and of Jews; but in the relation of Christians to the Roman empire of the first three centuries after Christ, it became patent. For, in Christ, man's direct access to God had been restored, and the more fully restored because it was not merely an individual, but a corporate access; it had become embodied no longer merely in the intuitions of individual mystics, but in the organic society of the Christian Church. Christ had come to save the world, but not, at least at this stage of His purpose, by the establishment of a new State, nor by any enlargement of the powers of the old State. His commission to His followers had been given in a series of magnificent,

and surely deliberate, contradictions: "all power is given to me . . .
go ye therefore and baptize"; "it is your Father's good pleasure
to give you the kingdom; sell what you have and give alms".
Such a commission assumed and, indeed, confirmed the continued
authority of the Roman world-State as the minister of an old
order which must co-exist with the new until 'the consummation
of the age'. Even when it became a corrupt and persecuting
Babylon, it must survive to be judged in the day of that consummation. For the first twenty years or so of Christian missionary
preaching, it had, on the whole, protected the nascent Church
from the mob law of Jews and Greeks. Even thereafter, even in its
worst days of active persecution, it was still the formulator and
enforcer of settled law – a law, after all, not very far from God's
law, however often it might be twisted or stretched by the despot
himself, or by his provincial governors, in their outbursts of
arbitrary power.[1] For that lawyer's task, the Church was essentially
unfitted by its very character as an elect body, living in a com-

---

[1] Religious persecution was not, of course, a violation of Roman law; it
was lawfully founded in the ancient and, till the emergence of Christianity,
obsolescent law of the Twelve Tables: "None shall have his own gods, nor
are new or foreign gods to be privately worshipped unless they be authorized
by the State". Yet to a primitive Christian, remembering the first commandment of the law of Moses, even this law, in its original intention, did not,
perhaps, appear to diverge far from the law of God. And a modern Christian,
with his wider historical knowledge, may feel compelled to admit that the
outlawry of strange worships seems to have been, in one form or another, a
necessary early stage in the establishment of the Moral State. From that early
stage Rome had advanced far – almost as far as the British empire in India in
the nineteenth century – on the road to universal religious toleration, subject
only to the requirements of public order. Its sole blunder had been to choose,
as its symbol of public order, a formality repugnant to all monotheists, the
worship of the emperors. Even so, a jurist might be puzzled to distinguish
this act of worship, in terms of mere law, from the modern American formality
of requiring school children to 'salute the flag', a practice which, though
specially repugnant to believers in theocracy like Jehovah's Witnesses, has
been recently judged by the Supreme Court of the United States to be a
legitimate exercise of State power. Of all freedoms, freedom from the exaction of unnecessary oaths is still, apparently, the most difficult even for the
most advanced States to guarantee.

munion of love beyond the law, and learning, in its worship and its acts of mercy, the exercise of spiritual powers which belonged to a future state of being: 'the powers of the age to come'. Nor, of course, could the Church claim that its members, thus living beyond the law, were in any sense above the law. The Church was, no doubt, as more than one modern Pope has claimed, 'the perfect society', but only in the sense that its members had seen perfection and knew their way to it. It was, no doubt, to use another modern Christian phrase, a 'redeemed society', but only in the sense that its members knew that the price of their redemption had been paid. Their emancipation was still to be accomplished and, meanwhile, though they had graduated from the education of servants to that of sons, they still needed the restraints of a master's discipline.

6

Such was the Christian idea of the State up to the beginning of the fourth century. It was, of course, profoundly shaken by the persecuting policy of emperors, for, in that, the State was clearly interfering with God's purpose of salvation and preventing the Church from carrying out its missionary commission. Yet, though shaken, the idea persisted. Tertullian could, indeed, write:

our hopes are fixed on the collapse of this world order and on the passing of the world itself into the day of the Lord, the day of wrath and retribution.[1]

and he could draw savage pictures of what 'retribution' would mean to persecutors and patrons of the amphitheatre; but he could write also, in words not less truly expressing the mind of the average Christian:

The Christian knows that his own God has given the emperor a dominion and needs must love and honour him and wish properity to

---

[1] *De Resurrectione.*

him and to the whole empire to the end of the world, *for so long shall it endure.*[1]

The events of the fourth and fifth centuries threw Christian thought off this balance and impelled it to seek a new one in the very different conception of a Christian world order. But before we describe that change, we must consider somewhat more fully the original philosophy of the Christian community during the first two and a half centuries of its existence. Our subject is the history of the State, not of the Church; but we shall not understand the curious mixed version of the Moral State that we call 'Christendom' unless we can regain a clear idea of 'primitive' Christian thought. We have to regain it, because the change in the character of the Church in the fourth and fifth centuries is the biggest single fact in European history. It is a fact so big that modern Europeans can hardly see it; it is so much the starting point of all their history that they can hardly see behind it. Behind it, behind the Church that baptized Clovis in 496 and thus launched the new stage in the adventure of the Moral State, they have generally no more than a vague impression of rude enthusiasts, as weary of the world as the devotees of pagan mystery cults and looking despairingly, like them, for the appearance of a supernatural Deliverer who should inaugurate a new Great Age. This short-sightedness has crippled modern thinking, for, in fact, the ideology of 'Christendom', whatever its merits, has been essentially a compromise with events, which makes sense only in the light of the much more coherent 'primitive' philosophy from which it was derived.

---

[1] Quoted H. M. Gwatkin, *Early Church History.* I. 190; Macmillan, 1927, our italics.

CHAPTER II

The beginnings of Christian thought

Original Christian idea of Church and State: the Economy of Grace and the
World Order – Primitive 'eschatology' and Augustine's conception of the
Reign of the Saints.

I

First and last, the original Christian philosophy was essentially a social one. Social irresponsibility is the very last
charge that can be made against primitive Christians. Indeed,
it is remarkable how little trace there is in their records of any
preoccupation with hopes of purely personal salvation or fears of
personal rejection. Theirs was a corporate life in which benevolence was, not only an individual duty, but a social necessity; the
whole society was organized for efficient mutual help in precisely
the same sense, and in the same degree, as it was organized for
common worship. 'Ministry of the word' and 'ministry to the
saints' were but two aspects of the same service; the bread and
wine of the primitive Eucharist were taken from the offerings
brought by the congregation for mutual support and for the
relief of the poor and sick.

This social activity did not spring mainly from philanthropic
precepts. In them, Christians could hardly claim any pre-eminence
over Stoics. It sprang from the intimate social character of the
Christian calling itself. In the language in which that calling was
first preached to the Jews, Christians were a 'people', a new Israel,
a Kingdom preparing itself to receive its King. They were being
"taken out of the nations"[1] to redress the failure of the old Israel,
to acknowledge collectively the Messiah whom the old had

---

[1] Acts 15. 14.

collectively rejected. At the very least, the new must be bound by the commandment given to the old: "There shall be no poor with thee."[1] But the obligation went beyond any mere relief of the poor. The old Jewish law had been keyed to the principles of social justice and brotherhood, and to the hope of an ideal social order. These principles and that hope had been the burden of much Old Testament prophecy, and had been focussed in the group of New Year ceremonies, which had been almost the central feature of the Temple worship: the Day of Atonement, ending with the Trumpet of the New Year and followed five days later by the rejoicings of the Feast of Tabernacles. In each fiftieth year, the new year thus ushered in was to have been the Year of Jubilee, "the time of the restitution of all things",[2] and that ideal of social liberation was reflected back on each annual act of worship. From that ideal and this symbolic worship much of the Christian language of 'redemption' was originally derived.

But, even so, this semi-political philosophy of the new Israel so understates the Christian sense of social unity as almost to misrepresent it. At a deeper level of thought, which came to be more and more clearly expressed as the gospel passed from Asia to Europe, the Church was, not so much a people or a kingdom, as an organic union; the Body of Christ, whose members shared the common life of His Spirit and moved in unison to the measure of His love. In that common life, if one member suffered, all suffered with it; in this "unity of the Spirit"[3] no man could live to himself; it needed no theory of communism to make each feel that all he possessed must be dedicated to the service of the brotherhood. Or as a modern scholar has expressed it,

the primitive Christians found the revelation of God in an historical figure so desperately human that there emerged within the early Church

---

[1] Deut. 15. 4.   [2] Acts 3. 21.
[3] Eph. 4. 8.

a faith in men and women so deeply rooted as to make modern humanitarianism seem doctrinaire and trivial.[1]

2

But, the modern critic may retort, all this was only the social conscience of a club. Christians held aloof from the social reforms of the Antonine era, from its schools, its public medical services and temple hospitals, its family allowances and benefactions for poor children, from all the "kindliness, generosity and goodwill"[2] of its municipal life. This abstention was thought, at the time, to betray a 'morose' temper, even a 'hatred of humanity'; does it look much better in retrospect?

It is easy to reply that abstention from the public life of the empire was forced upon Christians by the conditions of that life: by the aristocratic privileges and plutocratic standards of municipal politics, by the cruelty of public amusements and, above all by the idolatries which fenced all public activities. But these apologetic commonplaces are less than half the truth. Abstention – *egkrateia* – was one of the keynotes of Christian life and thought. In things otherwise lawful, it was not, indeed, the ascetic abstinence of "touch not, taste not, handle not"; but it was an absorbing concentration on a single purpose, and a withdrawal from distracting, and possibly dangerous, irrelevancies. That attitude did disable Christians from normal public life. Indeed, to some significant extent, it even disabled them from public testimony to their own beliefs. St Paul seems to have discovered this on his first arrival in Europe in the year 50. Shocked by his first sight of European society only nineteen years before the collapse of the Julio-Claudian empire in catastrophic civil war, he broke out at Athens into warnings of Christ's approaching judgement of the

---

[1] Hoskyns and Davie. *The Riddle of the New Testament.* Faber and Faber, 1931.
[2] Dill. *Roman Society from Nero to Marcus Aurelius.* Macmillan 1911.

civilized world.[1] This language still lingered on his lips when, a few months later, he wrote to his persecuted converts at Thessalonica.[2] But the mood passed during his residence at Corinth, as he later reminded his church there. He had left Athens with a sense of frustration, "in weakness and fear and trembling". His experiment in public prophecy had failed. His warning had been true, but it was not for him to speak thus to "the rulers of this age who are coming to naught". His business was the "demonstration of the Spirit and of power" to those who "have the mind of Christ". In all he subsequently wrote he devoted himself to that intimate task.[3]

This reconstruction of a particular incident may, perhaps, be questioned, but there can be no question of the general attitude of Christians at this period. They thought of themselves as 'sealed' or 'kept in wardship' for purposes alien to those of the existing world order – even as 'dead' and waiting for new life.[4] And it was this sense of special purpose that, above all, gave to Christian philosophy its social character.

In the Body of Christ lay the only hope for the human race. It not only lay there, but there it was being worked out and actually realized. For in Christ had been finally revealed man's only way of access to God. It was the way of a complete transformation or reconstitution of human nature, a *restitutio ad integrum*, a 'new creation'. The condition of progress in that way was complete self-surrender; its stages were a 'change of mind', a 'rebirth' to a new form of life and, at last, the full release of that life by the "emancipation of the body"[5], which must be refashioned into the likeness of the Risen Christ. And this hope of perfection

---

[1] Acts 17.
[2] 2 Thess. I. This passage is, it may be observed, the sole basis for much that has been written by modern critics about 'Pauline eschatology'.
[3] I. Cor. 2.
[4] Eph. 4. Gal. 3. 23. Col. 3. 3–4.
[5] Romans 8. 23.

was a corporate one: it was the organic and organized Church which was to grow into the "perfect man".[1] Today, when we have recast this language from its Greek original into Latinized theological terms – repentance, regeneration, resurrection – and have narrowed its application to a semi-legal conception of the 'salvation' of the individual soul, it is hard to recapture its vital meaning as describing an actual present process of communal life. But contemporary pagan critics took the point readily enough and met it, from the Platonic point of view, with an equally pointed denial. One such critic, writing about 178 in the last days of Marcus Aurelius, when the first barbarian invasion of Italy had been barely checked, and when the peril of the empire might well seem to demand the active service of every citizen, dismissed it as a frivolous dream.

Redemption is impossible. A man cannot change his nature; evil is inherent in matter and therfore a fixed quantity which cannot be diminished. . . . Return, then, to your obedience to the gods and your duties towards the emperor and your country.[2]

That was the issue and, plainly, it could not be compromised. Christians could not abandon the "economy of grace"[3] for a political world order which was "coming to nought". On such terms, as Tertullian said with his usual brutal exaggeration, nothing could be more alien to them than affairs of State. They would not, indeed, adopt a policy of positive non-co-operation; if they did that, as Tertullian also said, they had become, at the end of the second century, numerous enough to cripple the empire; but we today are in a better position than our fathers to understand how impossible it is for a totalist society to accept the limited loyalties which its quietest citizens are prepared to offer.

---

[1] Eph. 4. 13.
[2] Celsus. *True Word* – as summarized in Gwatkin, *Op. cit.* I. xi.
[3] Eph. 3. 2. 'Dispensation' is another Latinism which has almost lost all meaning today.

As we now know, under a system of total politics, mere quiet conscientious objection ceases to be harmless quakerism and is forced itself to become total. In a State organized under such a system Christians could expect, at best, to be but tolerated aliens and, sooner or later, the toleration was sure to be withdrawn. Their immediate expectation was, not so much any divine intervention which would bring them a spectacular victory over the world order, as a development of that order which would result in their expulsion from it. So Hermas about 140:

Look that, while you sojourn in a strange land, you get no more wealth than is barely sufficient for your needs; and, when its master comes to expel you for resistance to his law, be ready to leave his city and get you gone to your own, where you may live undisturbed and happy under your own law.[1]

3

It was this sense of choice between a society offering the sole hope for mankind and a society in decay, which could offer no hope at all, that gave to Christian philosophy its element of catastrophic urgency – its 'eschatological' element, to use the modern phrase. It was in this sense that 'the ends of the ages'[2] could be said to have come upon the Church and the world. The common modern idea, that Christians took little interest in ordinary life because Christ's imminent Coming must make any effective action impossible, is to put the emphasis in the wrong place. The point was, not that it was too late to save a dying society, but that it was futile to treat the patient for anything but the cause of his fatal disease.

The primitive preaching of Christianity did not so much predict a catastrophe as announce one. No future act of God or men could be as awful as those which God and men had just performed: the acts summed up in the words: "Jesus whom ye crucified,

---

[1] *The Shepherd*. First Similitude.
[2] I. Cor. 10. 11.

whom God raised from the dead"[1] God could, in a sense, do no
more: the 'day of salvation' had already dawned;[2] it remained only
for men, at this final parting of the ways, to choose between the
way of death and the way of life. It is remarkable how little direct
exposition there is in early Christian writing of the belief in the
'Second Coming'. It is rather referred to constantly as a matter of
course. Of course, those who choose the way of life must believe
in, and desire, its goal. There can be no sense of purpose without
an expectation of its accomplishment. Of course Christians looked
forward to Christ's full manifestation of Himself to the members
of His Body and their perfecting in His likeness. Their standards
of life and worship were the love of Him and the exercise of new
faculties derived from Him which were the 'gifts', but as yet only
the 'first fruits', of His Spirit.[3] They could not but be perpetually
conscious of

> Love too straitened in its present means
> And earnest for new power to set love free.

But the future to which they thus looked forward was hardly
separated in thought from the present which they already enjoyed.
It was by no chance that they spoke of Christ's expected return
in the same language as of His present nearness to the company
of believers: as a 'presence'. The language too, of a 'last time'
could be applied almost indiscriminately both to the age already
inaugurated by Christ's death and resurrection and to the deliverance still to be accomplished.[4] Both were parts of the same perspective. Moreover, the future itself was a perspective, rather than
a single 'end'; and, in so far as it was an 'end', it was, in the first
instance, the end of a present Church order, rather than of a
present world order. The 'day of the Lord' would introduce for
the Church a new economy, about the nature of which Christians
did not, on the whole, much speculate. It was enough that that

---

[1] Acts 4. 10.   [2] 2 Cor. 6. 2.
[3] I. Cor. 12. Rom. 8. 23.   [4] E.g. I. Peter 1. 20 and 1. 5.

K

day would vindicate the truth for which they stood and that, with the Risen Christ among them, the reality and power of His trans-natural life would be plainly revealed in them, for transmission to all men.

Two things only seemed certain about this new economy. One was that, however unearthly would be the means of its establish-ment, the scene of its establishment would be the earth. The Christian prayer was that God's Kingdom should come on earth; the belief that Christ would again be 'present' on earth was, as it were, the guarantee that it would so come. The prospect (to use the soldiers' slang of the twentieth century) of 'pie in the sky' after death might be the Christian's solace in danger or weariness or bereavement, but it was no part of his hope. Rather, he needed the assurance that the happy dead would not miss participation in the accomplishment of Christ's new creation on earth. Even in the ultimate vision of 'new heavens and a new earth', the Holy City was to come down to earth from heaven. This was the attitude of mind which has been obscured to the eyes of modern Christians by the false antithesis of 'worldly' and 'other-worldly'; the serious historian can have no use for that cant phrase of contemporary journalism.

And the other certainty about this new economy was that the transition to it must be marked by a 'judgement' – and a judge-ment of the Church, rather than of the world. At the dim end of that perspective, indeed, there would be a judgement also of the nations, but by the mildest test imaginable, the mere test of human kindliness; in contrast, in the foreground of the perspective, judgement would begin at the house of God itself, with the exaction of a much stricter account from its faithless stewards, its sleepy watchers, its slack servants.[1] On their readiness for that test must depend, humanly speaking, the whole timetable of God's purpose.

---

[1] I. Peter 4: 17. Matth. 24. 42 to the end of 25.

In short, it is a misunderstanding to attribute to primitive Christians anything in the nature of what is now called an 'ideology' – any vision of the future calculated to satisfy, at best, men's aspirations and, at worst, their appetites. They were committed to a personal relationship with Christ and a personal obedience to Him. In the perfecting of that obedience, in the development and consummation of that relationship, were summed up all their beliefs and all their hopes. About what might lie beyond that overwhelming personal commitment, speculation was felt to be almost indecent. Indeed, nothing could lie beyond it; Christ Himself was the End, and that Figure filled all the horizons of eternity.

4

Of course, there was speculation; but it was, on the whole, discouraged by the authorities of the Church. They discouraged it the more because it tended to concentrate upon the most material aspects of the perspective of the future, or rather, upon the two aspects which could most easily be given a material interpretation. The judgement and deliverance of the Church must, to some extent, impinge upon the world; and there must, apparently, be an interval between the end of the Church order and the end of the world order, during which Christ would visibly establish His Kingdom on earth. Both these ideas had been indicated in apostolic writings and it was easy to embroider them with the imagery, first of a divine vengeance upon an apostate Jewry and a heathen empire, and secondly, of a reign of the saints on the earth in a kind of Welfare State, hardly distinguishable from the old Jewish conception of a Messianic Kingdom or from the pagan mystery cult of a Great Age.

It was particularly this second sort of embroidery that seemed to threaten the integrity of Christian thought, because it tended to repeat exactly the attitude of mind which had led the old Israel to reject Christ, the attitude which translated the hope of human redemption into terms of politics – of 'mean things and mortal and things as they are'. It was in those words that, in the middle of the third century, Dionysius of Alexandria summed up his condemnation of 'chiliasm', of the ideology of Judaizing Christians who looked for 'a millennium on this earth devoted to physical well-being', instead of for

the glorious and truly divine appearing of our Lord and our rising from the dead, our gathering together with Him and our transformation into His likeness.[1]

And it was at this weak point that the original Christian philosophy was to give way under the impact of the events of the fourth and fifth centuries and was to be converted, by a curious twist of thought, into the new philosophy of 'Christendom'.

The author of that change, or at least its most powerful exponent, was Augustine, writing his *De Civitate Dei* in the years 413–16. Rome had fallen and her cataclysmic end seemed almost exactly to fulfil the prognostications of divine vengeance in which Christian speculators had indulged. Those unofficial speculators seemed to have been more nearly right than the official Church authorities who had expected the Roman dominion to endure until Christ's second coming. Might they not have been nearly right, too, in their other speculation about a reign of the saints? Had they, perhaps, been wrong only in supposing that such a reign must be preceded, as St Paul had seemed to predict, by the physical resurrection of "those who are Christ's at His coming"?[2] Had not St Paul also, in another place, bidden his converts to remember that they were already "risen with Christ"?[3] If so, must not the Church, as the City of God, assume, even now, all the practical cares of government, hitherto borne by the

---

[1] Eusebius, *Ecclesiastical History*. VII.
[2] I. Cor. 15. 23.
[3] Col. 3. 1.

fallen City of Rome? And so Augustine announced the conclusion that

the Church on earth is both the Kingdom of Christ and the Kingdom of heaven. The saints reign with Him now, though not as they shall do hereafter.[1]

This dangerous piece of 'realized eschatology' (to use another modern phrase) was to become the keynote of official Christian thought for the next 1,500 years. The Church which set itself, with so much success, to construct a Christian world order in Western Europe out of the rough material of barbarian tribes might almost be called a Chiliastic Church; it was, at any rate in a very real sense, an Augustinian Church, thinking of its mission largely in terms of government and organization, and not afraid to describe this necessarily makeshift work as the establishment of the Kingdom of God.

The novelty of this twist in Christian doctrine did not lie, be it repeated, in the belief that the Kingdom would be established on earth, but in the tacit assumption that it could be so established at a lesser price than 'the gloriously decisive change' for which earlier generations of Christians had so confidently looked. Augustine would doubtless have repudiated that assumption with horror; but, as we shall see in the next section of our study, it became, by the mere force of events, the dominant assumption of both Church and State in the new European society which was to call itself 'Christendom'. The Church of that society must regard itself as a Reigning Church, with at least viceregal responsibilities and powers.

---

[1] *De Civitate Dei* XX. 9. John Healey's translation 1610, (John Grant, Edinburgh, 1909).

IV

*The thirteen centuries of Augustine's
Reigning Church, 496-1789*

The preceding section having ended with the suggestion of a revolution in Christian thought in the fourth and fifth centuries, the following section opens with a sketch of the process by which this revolution worked itself out in Western Europe from the accession of Constantine to the time of Gregory the Great. Thence, an attempt is made to summarize the influence of this revolutionized Church on the political philosophy and practice of Christendom up to the eighteenth century. From the beginning, its mind was divided between two moods: the mood of direct participation in government as a means to the establishment of the Kingdom of God, and the mood of a 'holy communion' separated from the world of politics. Paradoxically enough, it was in this second 'other-wordly' mood, rather than in the first, that the Church most profoundly influenced political practice, and was able to create, at least in the British Commonwealth and the United States, a model of representative government which came near to embodying a distinctive Christian version of the Moral State. By contrast, in its political mood, the Church gave to Christendom an official philosophy of government which eventually crippled the efforts of reforming statesmen and exposed the State system of Europe to the subversion of the French Revolution.

According to this view, there is an ambiguity in the complaint, so often heard nowadays, that the Europe which has survived the two world wars is no longer a Christian society. It may be asked which of the two sides of Christendom's divided mind has been lost and which may have survived. That question can be answered only by considering afresh the history of the last century and a half.

CHAPTER 12

The beginnings of Christendom

Emergence of the Augustinian Church – Totalism of the Eastern Empire –
Roman Catholicism of Ambrose and Gregory: delimitation of jurisdictions;
the Church of Clerics; the Church of the poor; ambiguity of the Augustinian
philosophy; the new eschatology of the Day of Judgement.

I

Iin our analysis of early Christian thought and of its transition
into the Augustinian ideology, we have, of course, almost
recklessly foreshortened the history of five centuries. We must
now pause to get that history into perspective.

We have made the obvious point, which the modern world has
been inclined to blur, that the Western Church which led Europe
into the Christian stage in the adventure of the Moral State was
not the 'little flock' of the middle years of the first century, nor the
outlawed Church of the second, nor even the tolerated Church of
the years 260–303. Its idea of its mission in the world had significantly changed. But, in depicting the new venturer as the Augustinian Church, we have skipped a whole century of revolution.
The Augustinian Church was not the immediate child of the
early Church; its immediate parent was the Constantinian Church,
the Church which, in 314, emerged from its final decade of persecution under Diocletian, to become, almost in a moment, first,
under Constantine and his sons, the favoured religious agent of
emperors, and later, in the twenty-eight years from 363 to 391,
under successive emperors from Jovian to Theodosius, the trustee
of the official and only lawful religion of a Christian empire.

In Western Europe, this Constantinian Church, so suddenly
born, was to die as suddenly. After it had thus become, in the full

sense, an 'established' Church, its Western bishops had less than a generation in which to adjust themselves to their new status before its whole basis was apparently destroyed by Alaric's sack of Rome. They found themselves left overnight, like Daniel, as the sole heirs of the Babylon which had so recently promoted them to so much honour. It was from this double shock that the Augustinian Church emerged.

2

The transition was not, indeed, quite as abrupt as it appears, When, in 260, the Church emerged from the persecutions of Decius and Valerian, it was already a complex organization, weighted with institutional cares: with controversies about the terms on which its lapsed members could be re-admitted, with definitions of episcopal authority, with rules of discipline and with the deposition of heretical teachers. Already in 247–258 Cyprian of Carthage is recognizably the forerunner of a new line of states-men-patriarchs; already in 273 the church at Antioch found itself appealing to a heathen emperor to judge between two rival bishops. A personal faith in Christ was already beginning to give way to a defined faith about Christ; unity was ceasing to be a basic spiritual assumption and was becoming an institutional policy.

Still, the transition was abrupt enough. Church unity for the sake of the purity of its faith was one thing; Church unity for the sake of the cultural integrity of a world empire was quite another. Yet this was the overriding motive of Constantine and Theodosius, and the Church adapted itself to their policy with surprising readiness. Hence oecumenical Councils, summoned and managed by emperors; hence the elaboration of articles of faith to suit imperial policy;[1] hence a new impulse to denounce loose thinking

---

[1] The *homoousios* formula of the Nicene Creed – that the Son is 'of one substance' with the Father – was propounded by Constantine and reluctantly accepted by the Council of 325, most of whose members would have preferred a much more general statement and a much less elaborate credal unity.

as heresy, to drive heresy into schism and to treat schism as rebellion against a world order, rather than as personal apostasy from Christ. Never has a totalist policy led more directly to total disaster, for it was an attempt to base political on religious unity, and religious unity on the most insecure of all possible foundations: on assent to new intellectual definitions of absolute truth. In the hands of the emperors and patriarchs of Byzantium, who had three centuries in which to develop it, from Constantine's Council of Nicea in 325 to Heraclius' *Ekthesis* in 638, that policy destroyed the civilization of Italy and delivered a disrupted Syria and Africa into the hands of Arab invaders. That, in Western Europe, the experiment was so suddenly cut short in the fifth century by the fall, first of Rome, and then of Ravenna, was not a disaster but a merciful release. The Western Church was fortunate in being left to work out new relations with the State in barbarian Gaul, Spain and Britain. Justinian's temporary re-conquest of a devastated Italy in the sixth century accentuated, rather than weakened, the mistrustful independence of the Roman See; and the dawn of the seventh century, which in Syria saw Jacobites and Nestorians in league with Jews against the imperial orthodoxy of Constantinople, saw in a new Germanic West, from Toledo to Canterbury, something like a voluntary Catholic union under the mild Roman presidency of Gregory the Great.

3

We have called this Catholic Union the Augustinian Church, but, at the outset of its relations with the State, it derived its ideas, perhaps, not so much from Augustine's philosophy as from Ambrose's practical handling of imperial relations and, more generally, from memories of the fourth century in Italy and Gaul. Its ideas were as distinctively dualist as the ideas of the eastern empire were distinctively totalist; but it was an incoherent dualism, for there was a theological danger in working it out to any logical

conclusion. The characteristic heresy of those days was Mani-
chaeism, the theory of a dualist universe; and any assertion of a
dualism in God's choice of instruments for the working out of
His purpose in the world lay open to that damning imputation.[1]
One result of this was a tendency to turn the old contrast between
the two divinely ordained societies of Church and State into a new
distinction between two kinds of authority existing side by side
in the present world order: royalty and priesthood. Viewed thus,
the Church ceased to mean the whole body of believers and became
a hierarchy; and the distinction between it and the organs of the
State could be argued as a mere political problem of delimiting
jurisdictions.

The argument began as a claim by the Church to what would
now be called extra-territorial rights of person and property: thus,
about 378, when the validity of the election of a bishop of Rome
was in question:

in matters of faith and questions affecting their status, the clergy are
to be judged by their own peers,

and in 385, when Ambrose had been resisting the requisitioning of
a church in Milan:

what belongs to God is outside the emperor's power.

These claims to extra-territoriality were reinforced in the same
year by the scandal of Priscillian's execution for Manichaean
heresy at Treves. Here an emperor of Gaul, the usurper Maximus,
had intervened in a rather disreputable Church dispute in Spain,
and had taken judgment into his own hands. This portended
a worse totalism than any that Byzantium had yet dreamt of.

The next step in the development of Western dualism had
taken place in the preceding year 384, when Ambrose had for-

---

[1] Oddly enough, Christian socialism in England in the twentieth century
was to reproduce this bugbear. E.g. the late Dean of Lichfield in 1948, "The
contrast between sacred and secular . . . is now held to be false by all but a
handful of Manichaeans". F. A. Iremonger. *William Temple*, O.U.P.

bidden the emperor Valentinian, under threat of excommunication, to permit the re-erection of the altar of Victory in the Senate house at Rome. That veto (for it was no less) was based on the claim

that the ruler belonged to the Church otherwise than as a private citizen only; he was also, by virtue of his very office, a 'soldier of God', or, in later phraseology, the *advocatus ecclesiae*. This, again, implied, not only that it was his duty to protect the Church, but also that he was committed to the divine commandments in his political activity. If he ever felt himself in doubt as to his course, who else than the teachers in the Church could tell him what was the will of Almighty God?[1]

That this was no empty threat was shown fifteen years later when Ambrose actually excommunicated Theodosius for his massacre at Thessalonica. True, in these instances, the Church's claim to be the keeper of the State's conscience had been asserted only where the issues involved had been flat idolatry or inordinate cruelty; but it was only a step from this to the general principle laid down a century later[2] by Pope Gelasius I:

There are two powers by which this world is governed in chief: the consecrated authority of priests and the royal power. And of these the authority of priests is so much the weightier as they must render before the judgement-seat of God account even for the kings of men.

Here, then, we have already the main elements of that Western form of dualism which the mediaeval Church was to develop and in some degree to impose on the State: the immunity of the priest-hood from secular jurisdiction; its authority, at least in the last resort, over secular rulers; and, it must be added, its right to appeal to secular rulers for the suppression of heresy. For, though Priscillian's execution had shocked the highest authorities of the

---

[1] Lietzmann. *The Era of the Church Fathers*. B. L. Woolf's translation. Lutterworth Press 1950 p. 77. The two preceding quotations are from the same book pp. 55 and 79.
[2] c. 495.

contemporary Church, it was a precedent which might always be revived by later Churchmen who had forgotten the circumstances.[1]

These were the familiar elements of mediaeval clericalism; but it had another element which is too often forgotten. Constantine had found in the Church, not only a natural, but the only possible agent of the State for the relief of poverty. He had commissioned, and endowed, it to maintain and extend the institutions which its individual congregations had already established: hospitals, poorhouses, hostels for strangers, orphanages, homes for the aged; he had also entrusted to it, at least in some cities, the distribution of the State doles of grain. That tradition, too, passed to the Western Church. In a very real sense that Church was officially understood to comprise, not only the clergy, but the poor. So much so that, at the end of the eighth century, Charlemagne had to appeal to clergy and monks not to confine the education they offered to 'children of servile condition', but to extend it to 'the sons of freemen'. And when, much later, in the tenth and eleventh centuries, the bishops and councils of the French churches set themselves to mitigate the incessant petty wars of feudal magnates by the expedient of the 'truce of God', their repeatedly declared aim was to protect the property both of the clergy and of the poor and to preserve both from impressment into feudal levies. This policy was something more than mere charity for the destitute and the oppressed; the feudal system of France had deprived the peasant, almost as much as Roman law had deprived the slave, of any real citizenship in the State; he must find his citizenship, if at all, in the Church.

---

[1] It was not until 1215 that this doctrine was officially defined in the West by the Lateran Council. "Convicted heretics shall be handed over for due punishment to their secular superiors.... If a temporal lord neglects to fulfil the demand of the Church that he shall purge his land of the contamination of heresy, he shall be excommunicated."

4

Yet, behind all this delimitation of jurisdictions 'from precedent to precedent', lay a philosophy which did not wholly fit it – a dualist philosophy, but one which might be interpreted as merely a dualism of conflict between two incompatible totalisms. This was Augustine's contribution and it is this that justifies our phrase 'the Augustinian Church'.

We have already quoted Augustine's assertion of the Reign of the Saints as a present fact. He contrasted the peace of this City of God with the peace of the rulers of this world in language which almost suggested a flat contrast between good and evil, between those who should be saved and those who should be lost in the final Judgment. Yet, as Israel in Babylon had been commanded to 'seek the peace of the city' of their captivity, so also

during our commixture with Babylon, we ourselves make use of her peace, and faith does free the people of God at length out of her, yet so as in the meantime we live as pilgrims in her.[1]

Here was authoritative doctrine, but inevitably it raised two questions.

The first was: in a 'Christendom' whose rulers and citizens were baptized Christians, and Catholic Christians at that, what and where was the City of God, and what and where was Babylon? The temptation was strong to find somewhere a divine polity which was really distinct from the State and within which the saints could be really said to rule. And was such a polity difficult to find; was it not the hierarchy of priests and monks? And so the identification of the 'saints' with the priesthood and the 'professed religious', already prompted by the practical problems of jurisdiction, was confirmed by the philosophy of the greatest Father of the Church.

The second question went deeper. What was now the Church's

---

[1] *Op. cit.* xix. 26.

hope of emancipation from its 'commixture' with Babylon; what was the 'hereafter' of which Augustine had spoken, when the saints should more fully reign with Christ? To this there could now be only one answer. The Augustinian theory had flattened the old perspective of God's purpose. Already a century before Augustine, an Eastern bishop had publicly hailed the accession of Constantine as the coming of Christ:

> now again, the great Captain of the host of God, after the best soldiers of His Kingdom had stood the test of their full training ... has annihilated every enemy ... by His mere sudden appearing.[1]

This was, no doubt, mere rhetoric, prompted by the first intoxication of delivery from persecution; but now Augustine had soberly assured Christians that already "the kingdoms of this world are become the kingdoms of our Lord and of His Christ",[2] and that they were already sufficiently 'risen with Christ' to reign with Him. What remained, then, in the future but the terrors of the final Judgement Day? To the first Christians the 'day of the Lord' had not been primarily a Day of Wrath; but now, at the end of the sixth century, in the words of the best of Popes

> the end of the world itself has come near. ... Amid heavens ablaze and earth ablaze and elements flashing and crackling with fire, with Angels and Archangels, with Thrones and Dominations, with Principalities and with Powers, the tremendous Judge will appear ...[3]

It was, indeed, at this point that Christianity really succumbed to the imagery of apocalyptic extravagance which the modern world commonly associates with its primitive years. It was at this point, too, that Christian hopes and fears became narrowed to the prospect of individual salvation or damnation.

Such language came, no doubt, naturally to men facing, after

---

[1] Eusebius. *Ecclesiastical History* X. Eusebius' own speech at the opening of the restored Church at Tyre.

[2] Rev. II. 15.

[3] Gregory the Great to the Emperor Maurice, quoted from E. S. Duckitt, *The Gateway to the Middle Ages*. Macmillan, 1938.

so many successive calamities, the new incursion of the Lombards into Italy; and it remained natural during the next three centuries, as Arab invaders followed the Germanic, and Danish the Arab. But, spoken so long, it survived these Dark Ages, to become, from the eleventh century onwards, the settled language of mediaeval Christendom. Conceived in these terms, the prospect of the 'end' ceased to be a 'happy hope'[1] for the accomplishment of the divine purpose; more, it even lost any coherent connection with the Church's mission in the present 'day of salvation'. Almost inevitably, it degenerated into the nightmare that, some day, God would erupt into the work both of the Church and the world as horribly and irrelevantly as a volcano. If that were so, Christians must surely find their real hope, if at all, not in any future act of God, but in the success of the Church's mission here and now – which meant *ex hypothesi* the successful establishment of the kingdom of Christ on earth by the efforts of His ruling priesthood. So arose the mediaeval philosophy: the mission of the City of God was, not merely to convert Babylon, but to supersede or absorb it; the performance of that mission would be the key to all future history: the rise and fall of evanescent secular rulers would but confirm the triumphant progress of a Church destined, not only to inherit the heavens, but also to rule the earth. In such a philosophy there was evidently small place for a State distinct from the Church; and there would have been small hope for the dualism of the Moral State, if the Church's practice had not been better than its theory.

---

[1] Titus 2. 13.

CHAPTER 13

Christendom: The practice of government

Two histories of Christendom: the struggle for supremacy and the 'holy communion' – Creative influence of the 'holy communion' in government: monasteries and sects; the Christian congregation as the source of representative government in Britain and America – Philosophy of 'responsible' government – Development of English local government.

I

"In the most corrupt state of Christianity, the barbarians might learn justice from the law and mercy from the gospel. But the direct authority of religion was less effectual than the holy communion which united them with their Christian brethren in spiritual friendship." Thus Gibbon on the beginnings of the Christian State among the Teutonic invaders of the Roman Empire;[1] and, for a writer usually so insensitive to religion, the summary is surprisingly just. But, as we have seen, this holy communion entered on its new inheritance with a divided mind.

It had professed to be one of two Societies, each with its own distinct share in a single divine purpose: a body politic, responsible for bringing men into obedience to God's law of righteousness; and a body spiritual, responsible for bringing them under the operation of God's recreative power. That was still its profession, but now its official language had changed. As we have seen, almost in the hour of Clovis' consecration as a Christian king, it had pronounced itself to be one of two Powers, sharing the government of a single world order. It had asserted itself to be the senior in that partnership; and the time was to come when it

---

[1] *Decline and Fall*, Ch. 38.

would translate that assertion brutally into a claim to be, in its own right, the bearer of two 'swords':

Both swords, spiritual and temporal, are in the power of the Church; the one, indeed, to be wielded for the Church, the other by the Church itself; the one by the hand of the priesthood, the other by the hand of kings and knights, but at the will and sufferance of the priest. One sword ought to be under the other; the temporal authority must be subjected to the spiritual. . . . If the earthly power err, it shall be judged by the spiritual. . . . It is altogether necessary to salvation that for every human creature be subject to the Roman Pontiff.[1]

For thirteen centuries the Church was to hesitate between these two languages until the French Revolution transposed all political speech into a new key.

Unfortunately, of these two languages, the historian commonly has an ear for only one. Consequently, the history of the 'holy communion' has yet to be written. Instead we have only the history of the age-long rivalry between Western Church and Western State. That history is too familiar to bear repetition; let a few sentences suffice. It begins nearly 500 years after Clovis, with the crowning of Otto I as emperor in 962. By that act, the universal Papacy created the universal Empire as its protector against the anarchy of Italy. A century later it embarked on a struggle to keep its protector in subordination, on the declared principle that the 'Roman Pontiff' had the power to 'depose emperors' and to 'absolve subjects from their fealty to wicked men'.[2] In the course of the next two hundred years, the two universals fought each other into ruin; and from the ruin emerged the regional monarchies, each asserting against Rome its own autocratic claims to *Civil Dominion* and the *Divine Right of Kings*. In those claims they were powerfully abetted, from the sixteenth century onwards, by the divided post-Reformation Churches,

---

[1] The Bull *Unam Sanctam*, 1302.
[2] *Dictutus Papae*, 1075.

each seeking its own alliances with them, while a revived Papacy, now itself a regional monarchy with its own territory in Central Italy, began to speak in almost the same language, of absolute monarchy and territorial alliances. It did not abandon its universal claims, but, at least after 1648, it was willing to compromise them and even, on occasion, to discountenance the Jesuit Order which was their chief exponent. So, at the end of the 18th century, a chaotic Christendom of theocratic kings and political priests stumbled into the age of revolutions, fundamentally unprepared to deal with its problems.

2

This is true history, but it is surface history. If that had been all, the Christian form of the Moral State could never have given birth to the Christian conception of representative government. The greater truth is that, throughout these thirteen centuries, the heart of Christendom remained with the idea of the 'holy communion' – and that at a deeper level than Gibbon would have recognized; for it was the idea of a body spiritual, set in a world of, at best, static law and caring much for the moralization of that law, yet also set apart from it, to travail in the birth-pangs of a new creation which should transmute moral law into eternal life. It was to this pole that the Christian mind tended constantly to swing back; more, it was in this 'other-worldly' mood that, even by the test of worldly results, the Church did its most enduring work.

Hence that extraordinary movement of 'other-worldliness' which we tend to take idly for granted, without seeking to explain its attraction and its power: the monastic movement in the West, from its spontaneous beginnings to its extension into the preaching orders, over all its eight centuries from Martin of Tours to Francis of Assisi. To that movement the new West owed, not only its culture, the impulse of its education and the tradition of its art, its music and its scholarship, but also the very extent of its effective dominion and the basic standards of its government. At the turn of the eighth and ninth centuries, long before the struggle between Papacy and Empire had begun, Charlemagne's conquests fixed the territorial frontiers of Christendom in Central Europe; but the outposts of its civilization there, in such monasteries as those of Fulda and St Gall, had already been established by missionaries from Britain and Ireland, without political patronage or political motive. Thence, as the Dark Ages passed into the age of clerical civil services, the European tradition of orderly government, of administrative reform and institutional purity, was mainly created by successive religious orders, from the Cluniacs onwards; and, if Cluny became the driving power behind Papal pretensions, it was because those pretensions were themselves, in their origin, a genuine movement of reform, directed against the abuses of half-barbarous secular rule, only too faithfully reflected in laxity and disorder within the Church itself.

Hence, too, that later movement of revolt against a Church 'grown mad after temporalities',[1] which we take, no less idly, for granted under the blanket name of the 'Reformation'. There is a curious similarity, both of ideals and abuses, between the mediaeval succession of 'reformed' religious orders and the post-Reformation succession of 'reformed' sects, each seeking to realize more perfectly the conception of

a company of visible saints, called and separated from the world by the Word and Spirit of God, to the visible profession of the faith of the Gospel.[2]

It was, perhaps, only in Britain and in the British colonies in North America that this later manifestation of the 'holy communion' outlasted the wars of religion of the sixteenth and

---

[1] *Lollard Conclusions*, 1394.
[2] *Baptist Confession of Faith*, 1646.

seventeenth centuries and persisted into the 'age of Reason' in the eighteenth; but there its influence was so comprehensive that we hardly recognize it today for what it was. It is easy enough to see that we owe to it the growth of the missionary and reforming spirit which found expression in the Society for Promoting Christian Knowledge and the Charity School movement at the beginning of the eighteenth century, and in the agitation for the abolition of the Slave Trade at its end. But we owe to it also something else: nothing less than the main characteristics which, even in the reign of George III, and much more in the modern age, have differentiated English-speaking governments and political societies from those of the European continent: in particular, a system of Representative Government which is something other and better than democracy, and a Labour Movement which is something other and better than socialism.

Before, however, we consider the growth of representative government from this point of view, we must take note of the danger that lies in our use of the word 'reform'. It is the old danger of writing history too episodically, of emphasizing its novelties and ignoring what is permanent and unexciting. In these thirteen centuries, the 'holy communion' showed its vitality and its social effectiveness, not only in the mediaeval succession of Cluniac, Cistercian, Carthusian and Premonstratensian, but also and perhaps more powerfully, in the massive continuity of the Benedictine Order. So, too, in the seventeenth and eighteenth centuries, it showed itself less, perhaps, in the enthusiasms of English Dissenters than in the continuity of the English parish church; less, even, in the English Society for the Propagation of the Gospel than in the much older European Catholic missions in America, India and China. Indeed, in the history of slavery, the Spanish churches in Latin America may claim a more honourable, because a more consistent, record than English evangelicals. What follows should be read with these qualifications in mind.

3

Representative government of the British type is, perhaps, the most coherent attempt that has been made to solve the old problem of dualism in terms of politics. It has been an attempt to measure the exercise of political power by the ordinary man's sense of right and wrong. Its early history is that of a revolt against the totalism of absolute monarchy; but if the ordinary man measures right and wrong by what he thinks will contribute towards the strength and welfare of the State, the revolt loses itself in a vicious circle, and the State is half-way back to totalism. And if the citizens deliberately school themselves so to think, the State goes the rest of the way to a democratic totalism worse, because more unconscious, than that of absolute monarchy; for it has tampered with its own yardstick – nay, it has silenced its own conscience.

Paradoxically enough, therefore, it is of the essence of representative government that the public opinion which it brings to bear on political problems should not originate in political study. It should originate in groups formed for other purposes and living a life controlled by their own moral standards. If those standards are narrower than the standards proper to statesmanship, if they are no better than a moralization of self-interest – of the self-interest of landowners, merchants or artisans, for instance – the State will suffer; but, even so, a commercial or a trade union morality is, within its limits, a real corrective of political morality, and the resulting dualism is still substantially better than an uncorrected absolutism. If, on the other hand, the group standards are wider than those of politics, if they are standards of personal conduct (to put it in modern terms) which are as binding on an Englishman in an African village as on an American in his own home town, politics may come near to the ideal of the Moral State which the world has so long been seeking to realize.

Politics will come nearest to that ideal if the life and standards of the group are, in the full sense, religious. But here we encounter the old dilemma. As we have seen, the best religious standards of personal conduct cannot be directly translated into State policy. If representative government forgets this, it may relapse into another type of totalism, into the Puritan or Presbyterian theocracy which Englishmen, Scotsmen and Americans have all known only too well at different stages of their history. That dilemma is insoluble in theory, but the free citizen must be always solving it in practice for himself, if he is to remain free; in other words, it is soluble only before the tribunal of the individual conscience. The British solution has been simply to appeal to that tribunal, to focus both sides of the dilemma in the same persons, to give executive responsibility to the leaders of representative assemblies, and thus to change representative government into 'responsible' government. Englishmen did not discover that solution until the eighteenth century; indeed, as late as 1701 they had actually repudiated it; yet by 1814 it had become to them so much a matter of course that Castlereagh could condemn out of hand the Spanish model constitution, so dear to continental liberals, because it embodied 'the inconceivable absurdity of banishing from the legislature the Ministers of the Crown.'

If the British parliamentary movement owed its success in the eighteenth century to this discovery, it owed its strength in the seventeenth century to the religious character of the groups from which it sprang. James I was perfectly accurate, at the beginning of the century, in telling the House of Commons that it represented 'merely a private and local wisdom'; what he did not understand was that this very fact constituted its title to debate the policy of the State. Indeed, the more local the wisdom, the sounder the debate. The Scottish General Assembly was a better parliament than the Scottish Parliament itself, precisely because it was rooted in the parish kirk and, eventually, in the parish school; it strayed, in its bad days, into theocratic totalism in proportion as the presbyterian system became over-organized into district caucuses. In England a much less coherent presbyterianism led the Long Parliament similarly astray; its deviation into theocracy left the Puritan revolution to draw its main strength from the Independents, for whom the individual congregation was, in principle, the final unit of religious life.[1] That revolution failed largely because Independency found in Cromwell's New Model Army a more natural means of expressing itself than in Parliament. Congregationalism, in any of its many forms, necessarily adapts itself slowly to the representative system of a large region-State; it was not until nearly two hundred years after the Puritan revolution that Methodism made the congregational unit a power in the British Parliament, but then it created, in turn, both the Radical and the Labour parties.

In the seventeenth century, congregationalism came into its own, not in England, but in America. A very sceptical American, speaking in 1886 at the 250th anniversary of the founding of the First Church of Cambridge, Massachusetts, said that its founders "planted a congregational church, from which grew a democratic State". That is true. Sectarian distinctions apart, colonial conditions made the individual congregation the inevitable unit of group life; and Puritanism, which in England revolted against a Laudian Anglicanism, only to fall a victim to theocratic presbyteries, took naturally in the colonies a simpler congregational colour. With, it is true, one temporary interruption. The Colony of Massachusetts Bay passed through a dangerously totalist phase. But this phase, which modern historians tend to condemn so gravely, as if it were characteristic of all New England, was, even in Massachusetts, only a phase, lasting less than fifty years, from

---

[1] Hardly, perhaps, in principle. Congregationalism did not originally deny the idea of a universal church, though it rejected the universal authority of Rome; what it did deny was the idea of a national church.

1646 to 1691. It had been with hardly any serious intention of theocracy that in 1631 the charter corporation of the colony had originally admitted to "the freedom of this body politic . . . such as are members of some of the churches within the same". That, in itself, was the only possible basis for a representative commonwealth at the stage when townships were rudimentary and when the church congregation was the unit, not only of faith, but also of education and local administration. Later colonies were to have the same roots: the freer New England commonwealths of Rhode Island and Connecticut, the scattered settlements of the Plymouth Company in New Hampshire and Maine, and the Middle colonies of mixed population and religion in Maryland and Pennsylvania. It was by no chance that Connecticut devised for itself the first modern written constitution in 1639, or that Maryland passed the first Toleration Act in 1657.

4

Before we turn from the practice of government in Christendom to its philosophy, there is something more to be said about the practice of representative government. We have traced its roots to the fertilizing influence of the 'holy communion', but we must add something about its manner of growth.

There is a pathetic story that, in 1805, as Napoleon I watched his army march past on its way across Europe to Austerlitz, he was overheard to murmur: "*Tout cela ne vaut pas les institutions*". It is the purgatory of all serious dictators that they dream of political institutions, but fail to found them. It is, perhaps, Napoleon's sole title to exceptional greatness that, in the years of peace before 1805, he came nearer than any other of his kind to realize his dream, and that he turned his back on it with regret. The truth is that enduring institutions must have their own life in them; they cannot be founded and built up, they can only be sown and cultivated. Mere administration is the most evanescent of all human activities. Bagehot, in an essay contrasting the records of John and Henry Lawrence in India, marked it as the characteristic quality of 'middle-class' statecraft, in contrast to the 'aristocratic' instinct for 'evoking new power'. The historian may not find it easy to justify the use of these particular class adjectives; but he can be in no doubt about the truth of the contrast.

Belloc once described the peculiar quality of English society as "the quality which makes so many English things growths rather than instruments", and which has created

institution after institution . . . so lacking a complete fitness to its end, larger in a way than the end it is to serve and having, as it were, a life of its own that proceeds apart from its effect.

But if England is pre-eminent in this quality, it is not peculiar to her. The same quality may be seen in the mediaeval beginnings of a hundred institutions throughout Europe: in the free towns of the Hanseatic and Lombard Leagues, for instance, and in the forest cantons of Switzerland; or, if we turn to France, in the multiplicity of her local laws and *coutumes,* on the one hand, and, on the other, in the development, up to the early seventeenth century, of her *Conseil du Roi.* Nor did these beginnings die out with the Middle Ages; the local communities of France which compiled the *Cahiers* for the States-General in 1788–9 were not unready for the communal self-government which was to be the basis of the constitution of 1791, however inadequate that basis may have been for the national structure which the authors of the constitution sought to raise upon it. In our own day, there has been the same quality of independent vitality in the trade union movement throughout Europe and (to quote a very different example) in the German General Staff. There is, indeed, a dangerous romanticism about the modern cult of the 'spirit of England'. If England has been pre-eminent in developing this quality in her people, she owes her pre-eminence, not to some mysterious heredity, but to her deliberate choice of representative institutions for particular purposes at particular moments. For representative government must not only spring from living social groups; it must constantly be renewing them and constantly seeking new ones in which to strike fresh roots. Indeed (for, as usual, metaphor is inadequate) even agencies artificially created by such a government for its own purposes must be capable of growing to larger purposes. It is this chain reaction, so to speak, that marks the contrast between creative statesmanship and mere statecraft.

That contrast is the very stuff of European history. Statesmanship chooses for its institutions the very material which statecraft rejects as unsuitable. Witness, for instance, the contemptuous bewilderment of a Spanish ambassador describing England on the eve of the Elizabethan renaissance:[1]

This country is more fit to be dealt with sword in hand than by cajolery; for their are neither funds nor soldiers, nor heads, nor forces, and yet it is overflowing with every other necessary of life.

And *vice versa;* statecraft chooses what statesmanship rejects. Three centuries later, Lamartine, the romantic republican, was to magnify the French Revolution of 1848 as 'the accession of the masses to regular political power'.[2] It was in that blind alley that the revolution was to lose its original popular impulse and become a mere phase in the transfer of power to the middle classes. For a mass can never exercise regular political power. It has no life of its own. It must come to power either as a natural mobilization of living groups, or by being broken down artificially into *ad hoc* political parties; and its power will be immeasurably greater in the first alternative than in the second. In Britain, the political power of the Labour movement was to grow, not out of Chartism with its national Political Unions and Workingmen's Associations,

---

[1] Quoted from A. L. Rowse. *The England of Elizabeth* p. 394, Macmillan, 1950.
[2] *La Revolution de 1848.*

but out of the craft unions and the co-operative movement, out of groups in which the miners' lodge was hardly distinguishable from the Methodist circuit-rally.

This, however, is to run ahead of our story. At this stage we are not concerned with distinctively nineteenth century developments. A more relevant illustration of our point is the history of English county government. By the end of the fourteenth century, the decay of feudal jurisdictions left open a way to an extension of the central power of the monarchy; but the agency chosen by Edward III for that purpose was a local one. The Justices of the Peace were, from the first, the King's agents, but they were not his creatures; they were of the same breed as the knights of the shire who sat in parliament. They remained for two centuries predominantly an agency for 'law and order', and in that capacity they became in the sixteenth century the local field of battle on which, even more than on the central field at Westminster Hall, the Common Law of the English people won its victory over the Civil Law of the King's Bench.

The regiment of England is not a mere monarchy . . . for first it is not (the queen) that ruleth but the laws, the executors whereof be her judges, her Justices of the Peace and such other officers.[1]

In that local field, the Justices might be gentry, while the juries at Quarter Sessions might be men of an inferior class; but both were 'indwellers of the country' and it was difficult to set one against the other,

because the gentlemen will not meet to slander and deface the honest yeomen their neighbours.[2]

Thence, as a consequence of Tudor reconstruction, the Justices became a local executive, as well as a local judiciary – until, by the end of the eighteenth century, they were almost as much over-

---

[1] Aylmer. *An Harbour for True Faithful Subjects,* quoted A. L. Rowse, *op. cit.*
[2] Sir Thomas Smith. *De Republica Anglorum,* quoted A. L. Rowse, *op. cit.*

whelmed by administrative duties as their opposite numbers in France, the royal *Intendants*. They could not possibly undertake the additional duties entailed by the new Victorian reconstruction in the following century. When that happened, the central government had a new opportunity to supersede the local agency, if not, as in France, by a Napoleonic hierarchy of *préfets*, at least by central Boards controlling their own corps of experts. In fact, the pioneers of the Public Health movement, like Chadwick and Simon, did move in that direction. But the tendency was counteracted by another element in Tudor reconstruction: the rediscovery, so to speak, of the Parish.

No historian can now trace the process by which the parish, starting as an independent ecclesiastical unit within (though often coincident in area with) the primitive 'township' or manor, survived them to become the basic unit of local community life. Its survival seems to contradict much that has been written about the decay of the parish priesthood in the later Middle Ages; but, however that may be, the extraordinary fact is that the religious unit did survive the unit of primitive economics and rudimentary local administration. In the Reformation it became the local agent of the Royal Supremacy, carrying into effect 'the King's proceedings'. The constable became a parish officer; the churchwardens assumed new duties; till, at the end of the sixteenth century, the parish was made responsible, through its Overseers of the Poor, for the functioning of the Elizabethan Poor Law, and remained so for nearly 250 years. Like the Justices, it was clearly incapable of containing the new wine of Victorian reconstruction, but a sufficient Poor Law unit for another hundred years was found in a Union of parishes; and the later Sanitary Districts, School Boards, Standing Joint Committees and County Councils were created, in turn, after the same pattern of local self-government.

It was only at this latest stage that local authorities of all grades became formally integrated, by suffrage and polls, into the national system of representative government, but that change made comparatively little difference to their essential character. Their ancient predecessors had come into existence as representative institutions, and local opinion accepted and defended them as such; indeed, it was some time before elected Guardians commanded the same confidence as the Overseers whom they replaced.

Of course, especially at this latest stage, this deliberate enlistment of 'private and local wisdoms' in the service of the State had its danger: the danger that group loyalties might distort national service. This danger is probably at its worst when elected bodies are entrusted with executive patronage. The misuse of such patronage is, in fact, the specific disease of representative government; there is no better proof of the fact that private morality cannot be directly translated into public than the tragic process by which a good man's private sense of his duty to his neighbour is so easily transmuted into a system of political corruption. Still, politics is, at best, a dangerous trade, and this particular occupational disease, as British experience has shown, though exasperatingly recurrent as a minor infection, is definitely preventible in its grosser forms.

5

At the end of the eighteenth century, it became fashionable, both in England and America, to ascribe the discovery of liberal principles of government to the philosophers, rather than to the practical wisdom of ordinary men and women. 'Legislators', said a member of the Massachusetts Convention of 1788, 'have at last condescended to learn the language of philosophy.' Yet, to go no farther, Maryland's Act of Toleration preceded by thirty-two years, the publications of Locke's *Letter on Toleration*. In truth, both Americans and Englishmen were late in learning the language of philosophy, and it may be doubted whether it has done much good to either of them. Throughout the thirteen centuries of the Christian Moral State, the practice of government has always, for good or ill, marched ahead of its theory; and the unhappy history of its political philosophy accounts, in no small measure, for the unpreparedness of Christendom, at the end of the eighteenth century, to face the accumulated storms of the French and industrial revolutions. That is another story, which must have a chapter to itself.

CHAPTER 14

Christendom: The philosophy of government

Distortion of Christian political philosophy by the struggle for supremacy: transition from Covenant to Pact and Social Contract; the Moral State and Natural Law as sanctions of the *status quo* – The *status quo* of Europe in the eighteenth century; failure of reform movements – Burke's philosophy of the State – The Divine Right of Kings.

I

If, in the divided mind of the Augustinian Church, the 'holy communion' has been the source of the best political practice of Christendom, the ideology of the *Civitas Dei* has been the source of much of its worst political philosophy. The degeneration of its philosophy was the worst and most lasting effect of the conflict between Papacy and Empire.

In particular, this conflict diverted the doctors of the mediaeval Church from the study of the origins and nature of the Moral State to what seemed a more practical study of the circumstances in which subjects might lawfully rebel against their rulers. This dangerous attempt to deduce a rule from its exceptions (for none doubted that obedience to duly constituted authority was the rule) led them to shift the emphasis of their political philosophy from the idea of a Covenant made by a people and its governors with God to the very different idea of a *pactum* between governor and people.

This shift was the more natural because the early Teutonic conception of the 'oath of fealty' partook of the nature of a pact. If at first it was a one-sided pact, the growth of feudalism increasingly encouraged the idea that it was a mutual one between king and vassals, binding only so long as the relation of 'true lord' and 'true liege' should be observed by both parties. When the Church doctors came to formulate a philosophy on this basis, and to apply it, not to any feudal relationship, but to the obligations of the whole body of citizens, Aquinas, with his usual candid common sense, doubted at first whether the existence of such a pact could be postulated of all political societies. But his later teaching was more dogmatic and, three hundred years later, Suarez had no hesitation in quoting him in support of the general proposition that

the Prince has that power of lawgiving which the people have given him.

This was a strictly accurate statement of mediaeval theory and practice, but 'law-giving' is not the whole of government. The Emperors had ruined Germany by their Italian adventures without changing its laws. Suarez was a Jesuit of singularly independent mind, and his statement did not necessarily limit the executive authority of governments; but the members of his Order, intent on the propaganda of the Counter-Reformation against heretical kings, extended the argument until they came near to making themselves the pioneers of the later revolutionary gospel of popular sovereignty; for it was they who first whole-heartedly argued that, while priests derive their authority from God, princes derive it *only* from their people.

Thence, almost imperceptibly, the Covenant came to be generally regarded as a pact, not even between prince and people in an already constituted State, but between individual men as the founder members of a State. As thus:

All public regiment of what kind soever seemeth evidently to have arisen from deliberate advice, consultation and composition between men judging it convenient and behoveful.[1]

In that context, it became easy to regard any constituted authority, not even as the people's representative or trustee, but merely as

---

[1] Hooker. *Ecclesiastical Polity.*

their temporary servant or agent, holding office at the people's pleasure. Thus Dryden's satirical portrait of a Whig in the days of Charles II:

> He preaches to the Crown that Power is lent,
> But not conveyed, to Kingly Government.

So was born the theory of the *Social Contract*, a theory lacking any historical basis, but infinitely adaptable as the justification of almost any political change, from the constitutional revolutions of England and America to the French democracy of 1789.[1]

With this went an even worse distortion of the very idea of the Moral State. The mediaeval doctors found in their master, Aristotle, the idea that

Virtue must be the serious care of the State, for (otherwise) the community becomes a mere alliance which differs only in place from alliances of which the members live apart, and law is only a convention, 'a surety to one another of justice', as the sophist Lycophron says, and has no real power to make the citizen good and just.[2]

But the doctors could not swallow this high doctrine of the *Regnum*, which seemed to trench too far on the functions of the *Sacrum*. They preferred the sophist view which Aristotle had condemned; and they converted his idea of the State as a *koinonia*, a fellowship whose end is virtue, into the idea of a *commune bonum*, a Common Good which is the end of all just government. And they found themselves obliged to define that Good in very modest terms. They would hardly have assented to Bentham's definition of it as simply "the attainment of pleasure and the avoidance of pain"; but their own conception of it was not much more exalted. Charlemagne might interpret his subjects' oath of fealty as a promise that each of them

of his own accord should strive, according to his intelligence and strength, wholly to keep himself in the holy service of God;[3]

---

[1] Hobbes' version of the Social Contract led, of course, to a different conclusion, but he stands apart from the main line of development.
[2] *Politics* III. 9.   [3] Capitulary of 802.

but, in Christian doctrine, virtue, in any full sense, could be attained only be regeneration, which was the Church's sphere; it was enough for the State, especially in days when European Christendom was still struggling out of the Dark Ages, to preserve its citizens from the gross evils of breach of contract, robbery and violence.

But, as European civilization advanced and as its political philosophy became secularized, this modest view of the State tended to degenerate into something very like pure materialism. Secularization reached a point where, for all practical purposes, the *sacrum* disappeared as an independent partner of the *regnum*, and yet, except in terms of mere power, the *regnum* was not expected to take over any of its duties. Locke's statement, for instance, that "government has no other end but the preservation of property", whatever its truth when combined with other truths, was too dangerously comfortable a doctrine for Whig landlords in the eighteenth century and for ten-pound householders in the nineteenth. Locke, indeed, defined 'property' as "life, liberty and estate"; but, even so, the static word 'estate' is in significant contrast with the later American version, "the pursuit of happiness". It recalls Gibbon's calm statement of the Whig assumption:

Such is the constitution of civil society that, whilst a few persons are distinguished by riches, by honours and by knowledge, the body of the people is condemned to obscurity, ignorance and poverty.[1]

All such statements, indeed – even Bentham's "evil is pain or the cause of pain; good is pleasure or the cause of pleasure" – are wrong, not in what they assert, but in all that they omit.

2

The jurist's conception of a Law of Nature had much the same history of degeneration, and declined into the same starveling

---

[1] *Decline and Fall*, Ch. XV.

thinness. The mediaeval canonists derived it partly from the Roman Digests, but partly also, it may be suspected, from the first chapter of the Epistle to the Romans; and their conception of it retained something of the grandeur of St Paul's vision of God's revelation of His moral law through nature even to pagan man. It retained, too, something of the radicalism of the later Roman jurists who, on occasion (as in the case of slavery), could conceive of Natural Law as setting a higher standard than either the law of Rome or the law of nations. But when the post-Reformation fathers of international law set themselves to deduce from *Right Reason* some standards to which the regional States of a disrupted Christendom might be expected to conform, they could regard the Law of Nature only as a greatest common denominator of State laws. Thus, in the words of the first and greatest of them:

To this Law (of Nature) belongs the rule of abstaining from what belongs to other persons; and, if we have in our possession anything of another's, the restitution of it, or of any gain which we have derived from it; the obligation to fulfil promises; the reparation of damage occasioned by negligence; and the recognition of certain things as meriting punishment among men.[1]

This, again, except for the last clause, amounts to no more than the preservation of the *status quo*, especially in the distribution of property. It would not be easy, for example, to deduce any theory of fair taxation from Locke's definition of the purposes of the Social Contract, or from Grotius' Dictates of Right Reason. Still more difficult would it be to deduce from them a justification of such social legislation as the Elizabethan Poor Law; yet no act

---

[1] Grotius. *De Jure Belli ac Pacis*. He went on, it is true, to derive all 'civil rights' from the Law of Nature, because civil society must be assumed to arise from a 'mutual compact', of which natural law requires the observance. But if this means that men may freely contract to transgress the bounds of the Law of Nature, it goes too far and would justify any tyranny by the fiction that it had been originally authorized by a binding contract; while, if it does not mean that, the argument tends only to give to 'civil rights' an august pedigree, while still restricting their scope.

of policy was ever more clearly justified, by the broad principles of moral purpose and popular consent, than this legislation, passed as it was by the constitutional representatives of the people after years of pioneering municipal experiment in the relief of destitution and infirmity.

At this point, indeed, the philosophy of the *respublica Christiana*, swinging back full circle, had come almost to reproduce the very characteristic for which, some fifteen centuries before, Christians had condemned the bankrupt *respublica Romana*. Rome, wrote Augustine, in spite of the fine language of Scipio and Cicero, "never had a true commonwealth", because it never had a just rule of law, applicable to a whole people, and therefore

no society united in one consent of law; therefore no people, no estate of the people, but rather of a confused multitude, unworthy of a people's name.

It had a commonwealth only in the lower sense of

a multitude of reasonable creatures conjoined in a general communication of those things which it respects.[1]

No more could be postulated of the Social Contract State, bound to the observance of the Law of Nature. The things which the multitude 'respected', and could be presumed to have created a common government to secure, could be nothing more than their immediate material interests. To quote Dryden's satire again,

> . . . Interest never lies;
> The Most have still their Interest in their eyes;
> The Power is always theirs, and Power is ever wise.

It might almost be said of such a State, as de Tocqueville said of Napoleon I, that it could be "as great as a man can be without virtue".[2]

This is not to say that these prophets of an almost sub-moral

---

[1] *De Civitate Dei.* Book XIX.

[2] It may be worth remembering the dictum of Montesquieu, that the motive power of a monarchy is not 'virtue', but the sentiment of 'honour'.

State may not have been wise in their generation. For, in the seventeenth and eighteenth centuries, Christendom had lost its essential dualism. National churches, Protestant and Catholic, had become domestic chaplains to the State; their ministers were half on the throne and had admitted kings half-way to their altar. The time was to come when this close alliance would end, when the State would rise and cast out the Church. That is the history of the 150 years after 1789. But, meanwhile, what tyrannies might not be born if the allies sincerely tried to realize the ideal of the Moral State under these conditions? To answer that question, we have only to look at the history of the Scottish Covenants; of the European policy which, in the hands of the Emperor Ferdinand II, devastated Germany in the Thirty Years War; of Laudian reform in England; of France under Louis XIV and the Gallican Church – in a word, at the whole history of the seventeenth century. In such days, was not a meagre minimum of State morality, perhaps, the necessary guarantee of the sobrieties of government by popular consent and of its incarnation in the supremacy of agreed and accepted law? And, in the Church, were not the dry moralities of the official Anglican pulpit in the eighteenth century, so despised in Scotland, the better preservative of the essentials of the Moral State? Did they not, at least, as the Duke of Wellington once said, make England "a nation of honest men"?

3

But, after all such allowances have been made, the historian's final verdict must be that, in the second half of the eighteenth century, when, on the eve of the Revolution, a generation of liberal statesmen set themselves to reconstruct the old State system of Europe, this meagre political philosophy contributed powerfully to their failure.

We have already noticed the thirty years after the Seven Years

War as a period of peace; it was also a period of attempted reform. It was heralded by a new movement in political thought, away from abstract theory towards a 'positive' study of the facts and historical growth of political societies. Its pioneers were Montesquieu, whose *Esprit des Lois* had been published in 1748, Diderot, whose *Encyclopédie* had been first launched in 1751, and Quesnay whose *Tableau Economique* appeared seven years later. There followed, in 1764, the first year of the peace, Beccaria's *Crimes and Penalties* and, six years later, Turgot's *Letters on Free Trade in Cereals* and Howard's report on prison conditions in England. Filangiere's *Science of Legislation*, marked the latter days of the period in 1780–85; but before that the year 1776 had seen the publication of a trinity of remarkable works: Boncerf's *Feudal Rights*, Bentham's *Fragment on Government* and Adam Smith's *Wealth of Nations*.

If all this new marshalling of thought gave so little immediate impulse to statesmanship, the reason for its ineffectiveness was largely that it was radical only in its detection of abuses and that, in its political ideas, it reproduced almost slavishly the timid conservatism of the theorists whom it professed to despise. To Adam Smith, for instance, the proper expenses of government to be defrayed out of general taxation, were still primarily "the expense of defending society and that of supporting the dignity of the chief magistrate"; and it is difficult to detect any moral content in his use of the word 'improvement', as applied to political society.[1] To Montesquieu the first virtue of government was 'moderation', to be secured by a system of checks and balances. The ideal type of such government was the English; but, however he might hate the corruption of the French system under Louis

---

[1] The *Wealth of Nations* does not, of course, embody Adam Smith's political philosophy; for that he had designed a companion work. Even so, it is possible to find in it the germs of a policy of moral reform. But the fact remains that its influence, outside strictly economic issues, could not, in its day, be other than conservative.

XIV, the balances of hereditary and professional privilege seemed to him better than none. "If", he wrote, anticipating Burke by nearly half a century,

If in a monarchy, you abolish the prerogatives of landowners, clergy, nobility and towns, you will soon have either a popular or a despotic government.

All this was, of course, to miss the point of the European problem. The time for moderation was past; no expenditure will defend a society which has ceased to be morally defensible; the reform of abuses – the humanization of the criminal law, the liberation of trade from a stifling system of taxation, even the very restoration of government solvency – had become impossible, as Calonne reported to Louis XVI in 1786, save through a comprehensive policy which should

re-animate the whole State by remoulding everything which is vicious in its constitution.

But, by the standard of the still accepted philosophy of the age, the dilemma of such reconstruction was insoluble. Over all the continent of Europe, it must entail the drastic diminution, if not the abolition, of four sorts of privilege: feudal, ecclesiastical, municipal and official – official in the sense of all the vested interests of old government machines, from the Parlements of France and the mediaeval Estates of Sweden to the tax farmers of Naples. The common vices of all Europe which had to be 'remoulded' were the fiscal immunities of the nobility, the Church and the municipalities; the personal servitude of the cultivator and his triple burden of royal taxation, feudal dues and ecclesiastical tithe; and the strangling of trade by tolls, monopolies and arbitrary regulation of prices. But all these evils were bound up with accrued rights of property, or vested commercial interests, which the State, according to current philosophy, existed primarily to defend and perpetuate. It was by no chance that reforming philosophers found, in these years, their only escape from this dilemma by concentrating on the one kind of reform which was uncomplicated by respect for property rights or a hankering after prudential restraints on despotism; the reform of the criminal law. It was by no chance that, in all else, they had to leave the field of political philosophy to a rival school of theoreticians who distilled a new radicalism from old doctrines in Morelly's *Code de la Nature* (1755) and Rousseau's *Social Contract* (1760).

4

Where philosophy failed, statesmen failed too. In the opinion of contemporaries, fundamental reform was overwhelmingly urgent by the crudest and simplest of tests. Europe, they believed, lived on the brink of starvation. Famine was a common experience. The dearth of the 1780s in France recalled the nightmare of the last war years of Louis XIV when, from 1689 to 1715 on Taine's estimate, one-third of the peasantry had died of hunger. Arthur Young reported that French agriculture was at the stage of the tenth century and, if that was an exaggeration for France, it was hardly an exaggeration for southern and south central Europe. Montesquieu described the peasantry of the rich plains of Lombardy as having "become feebler, their face leaden, their body unhealthy". "What nation of Europe", wrote Filangieri, "does not see a half, or at least a third, of its soil uncultivated?" and he went on to describe the labourers of the typical baronial estate in Italy as "condemned to the most horrifying misery. You will see indigence portrayed in their face; you will see it in their very bed". In the Tuscan Maremma, tillage and population were both declining. In France d'Argenson quoted a parish where "there are thirty young men and women of more than marriageable age; but there are no marriages, they do not even think of it". Pombal recorded that, on the Douro, "the cost of cultivation is greater than the value of the produce; the general and extreme poverty has caused the habitual prostitution of the daughters of the vine

growers." Joseph II returned horrified from a glimpse of peasant
conditions in Bohemia; a contemporary described them as worse
even than those of Hungary.

Yet in face of this urgency the reforming statesmen accomplished hardly anything. Their two achievements were the great
Prussian Law Code of 1791 and the suppression of the Jesuit
Order in 1773. The first marked the same way of escape into
reform of the criminal law as we have noticed among the philosophers; in the second, statesmen had the philosophical support
which they lacked elsewhere, for the old fourteenth century
doctrine of *Civil Dominion* had been revived with great power by
a German scholar, Febronius, in 1763, in his *Status of the Church
and Legitimate Power of the Roman Pontiff*. That was an ominous
reminder that, of all forms of privilege, the ecclesiastical was the
least strongly entrenched; yet from the point of view of reform,
the temporary eclipse of the Jesuits destroyed as much good as
evil; it strengthened the hands of centralizing kings, but it
weakened the education of the people. For the rest, the strongest
of the reforming statesmen, Pombal in Portugal and Gustavus III
in Sweden, could do little more than increase the immediate
power and resources of the State by breaking the nobility and the
Church. Others, like Tanucci in Naples and Floridablanca in
Spain, left a name only for fragmentary reforms or great public
works. Joseph II tried to do everything in five years and achieved
only a mountain of paper and a revolt in the Netherlands. The
best of them all, Turgot, was broken by the defenders of privilege
after no more than twenty months of power; the least honest of
them, Catherine II of Russia, did no more than leave a record of
grievances in the *Nakas* prepared for her abortive Commission of
1767–9. The most successful were those who worked in a small
field; Bernstorff in Denmark, Leopold in Tuscany, Du Tillot in
Parma and, at least in the matter of peasant emancipation, the
Sardinian kings. It was this spectacle of impotent governments,

not any experience of their tyranny, that lent point and force to Rousseau's explosive epigram that man had been born free, but was everywhere in chains. In this deadlock of vested interests, it became easy to believe that the State itself was the source of human imperfections, that "error is principally indebted for its permanence to social institution".[1] Hence the two master-impulses of the coming age of revolution, in all its phases; a pathetic belief in 'liberty', as the essential but sufficient condition of 'human perfectibility', and a blind search for a system of government which should be strong enough, not to construct, but merely to abolish.

5

Fortunately, Christendom was not left to enter the new age quite without any other political belief than this negative one of the Immoral State, which was eventually to find its logical prophet in Marx. England, with its very different social experience,[2] began, on the eve of the Revolution, to express in words, as it had long expressed obscurely in its practice of government, a more positive conception of 'civil freedom'.

Edmund Burke, who was its chief formulator, has been, until quite recently, almost persistently misunderstood. His party pamphlets have been taken as sound history, while his anti-revolutionary philosophy has been dismissed as a crotchet of old age and declining powers. This is almost the exact reverse of the truth. Burke was a Whig partisan, no more reliable as a witness to contemporary fact than any other party politician. But, as other such politicians have not seldom been shocked into statesmanship by war, he was shocked into philosophy by, first, the American and, then, the French Revolution.

---

[1] Godwin. *Political Justice*. 1793.

[2] Except, indeed, in its government of Ireland. It is well to remember that in 1787 Lord Clare's judgement of conditions in Munster was no different from those we have quoted for the continent of Europe: "It is impossible for human wretchedness to exceed that of the miserable tenantry of that province."

It would be near the truth to say that his philosophy began and ended in the re-vivification of the two ancient ideas of dualism and of covenant. As in the contemporary American re-statement, the ideas were secularized, but not de-moralized. No less than Montesquieu, he appealed from theory to experience:

Civil freedom ... is a blessing and a benefit, not an abstract speculation; and all the just reasoning that can be made upon it is of so coarse a texture as perfectly to suit the ordinary capacities of those who are to enjoy, and those who are to defend it.

In those terms, as with all the "duties or satisfactions in life", "liberty must be limited in order to be possessed"; but it is also "a good to be improved, not an evil to be lessened". For

it is not only a private blessing of the first order, but the vital spring and energy of the State itself, which has just so much life and vigour as there is liberty in it.[1]

On the other hand, liberty alone does not make the State. The State, of course, like the family, originates in voluntary agreement, but the originating agreement does not exhaust the duties of citizenship, any more than it exhausts the duties of marriage and parenthood. "The choice is voluntary, but the duties are not matter of choice. They are dictated by the nature of the situation". Moreover,

we have obligations to mankind at large which are not in consequence of any voluntary pact. They arise from the relation of man to man, and the relation of man to God, which relations are not matter of choice. On the contrary, the force of all the pacts which we enter into with any particular person, or number of persons among mankind, depends upon these prior obligations.

As children, without their own consent,

come into a community with the social state of their parents, endowed with all the benefits, loaded with all the duties, of their situation ... so, without any stipulation on our own part, are we bound to that relation

---

[1] *Letter to the Sheriffs of Bristol*, 1777.

called our country, which comprehends (as it has been well said) 'all the charities of all'.[1]

And thus the argument proceeds to that rhapsody on the State, so hackneyed by quotation, but so rarely quoted with any appreciation of its pointed contrast with the sub-moralities which had so long done duty for political philosophy in Christendom:

Society is indeed a contract. . . . It is not a partnership in things subservient only to the gross animal existence of a temporary and perishable nature. It is a partnership in all science, a partnership in all art, a partnership in every virtue and in all perfection. As the ends of such a partnership cannot be obtained in many generations, it becomes a partnership not only between those who are living, but between those who are living, those who are dead, and those who are to be born. Each contract of each particular State is but a clause in the great primeval contract of eternal society, linking the lower with the higher natures, connecting the visible and invisible world, according to a fixed compact sanctioned by the inviolable oath which holds all physical and all moral natures, each in their appointed place.[2]

6

It may appear eccentric to have carried a discussion of pre-revolutionary philosophy thus far without any mention of the cult of absolute monarchy. But, in truth, that cult was always a side-track and it had become clear enough, long before 1789, that it led into a blind alley. As a philosophy, it belongs rather to the nineteenth century reaction against the revolution. At this stage in our study, therefore, it hardly calls for more than a footnote.

As originally asserted in the fourteenth century, the Divine Right of Kings meant merely the divine right of secular government. It was the region-State's version of the general doctrine asserted by the Empire against the Papacy:

The imperial dignity and power has proceeded from of old directly

---

[1] *An Appeal from the New to the Old Whigs*, 1791.
[2] *Reflections on the Revolution in France, 1790.*

from the Son of God, and God has plainly given laws to the human race through the emperor and the kings of the earth.

As such, it was as much a doctrine of constitutional law as of personal authority: the law of election in the Empire; the Salic law of male hereditary succession in France.

The emperor is made true emperor by the election of those to whom it appertains and needs not the confirmation or approbation of anyone else.[1]

It was not until the seventeenth century that monarchy came to be regarded as a divinely ordained institution, as against any alternative form of government, in the same order of ideas as that in which episcopacy was regarded as a divinely ordained institution in the Church. Even then, the view was at first little more than a pulpit rationalization of national facts: in England, the legal recognition of the sovereign, since 1559, as "supreme governor of the realm ... as well in all spiritual things or causes as temporal"; in France, the historical record of her kings as the creators of national unity. It hardly became a general doctrine in either country until it was embodied, in 1680 and 1685, in Filmer's theory of 'fundamental hereditary right' and in Louis XIV's assertion of his absolute prerogative by the revocation of the Edict of Nantes. As an effective theory of government, it died almost as soon as it was born. In England its single result in the eighteenth century was the Jacobitism which stultified the only possible opposition to Whig oligarchy, both in Church and State, and postponed, for almost a hundred years, the growth of a two-party system in parliament. In France it did more to set a precedent for the revolutionary assertion of unlimited popular sovereignty than to strengthen the hands of royalty. Nowhere in Europe, as we have seen, did it arm rulers with any power to reform their States.[2]

---

[1] Diet of Frankfurt, *Licet Juris*, 1338.
[2] Except, perhaps, in Prussia. The German version of Divine Right goes

Yet its influence did survive in two ideas. One, from which we still suffer, is the indivisibility of sovereignty. This was an embroidery by Hobbes on Bodin; it, too, is no older than the seventeenth century. It was not an idea confined to monarchy; but it was appropriated by monarchists to re-inforce the claim to absolute divine right, for (as with the plebiscitary dictatorship of democracy) indivisibility can most appropriately be embodied in a single person. Thence it was transferred later to the sphere of international law, where it has acquired a mysterious prestige as the supposedly indispensable foundation of national independence.

The other legacy of the Divine Right of Kings is a peculiarly English one. In the mind, though by no means always in the practice, of Charles I, Divine Right remained a constitutional idea: the idea of a king as a divinely ordained guardian of national laws, enacted with the people's assent, and therefore of a national Church established by law. There have been many worse ideas of government than those contained in Charles' alleged advice to his son, and, if the words are not his, it is no less significant that his devotees should have put them in his mouth:

I cannot yet learn that lesson . . . that it is safe for a king to gratify any faction with the perturbation of the Laws, in which is wrapped up the Public Interest and the good of the Community;

and

Never charge your Head with such a Crown as shall by its heaviness oppress the whole Body (of the realm), the weakness of whose parts

---

back further as a doctrine than any other national version. It goes back to the teaching of Luther himself and, within ten years of Luther's death, it became, by the Peace of Augsburg, the legal title of the Lutheran Church to exist in Germany, on the recognized principle that a people's religion is what their ruler pleases. And, though Frederick the Great's power was principally rooted in a barely religious tribal loyalty, Lutheran preaching did something to enhance it. Germany is the land of exaggerations, which other lands find indigestible.

cannot return anything of strength, honour, or safety to the Head, but a necessary debilitation and ruin. Your Prerogative is best showed and exercised in remitting, rather than exacting, the rigour of the Laws, there being nothing worse than a legal Tyranny.[1]

Of course, this last idea contained a fallacy. Since political constitutions were first devised, men have sought for some authority which might embody, as it were, the restraining conscience of the State. Of such are the American Supreme Court and Siéyés' device of a National Jury. But it is almost a contradiction in terms to locate the national conscience in the holder of supreme executive power; the prerogative of remitting law (as James II was to find) cannot be entrusted to an authority whose primary function is to enforce the law. A king can become, in his own person, the guardian of the national conscience only by ceasing, in his own person, to be the author of national policy. Today, however, under the British system of representative government, he has so ceased, and the Crown has, in fact, tended to become the national fountain of honour, in a deeper sense than as the dispenser of honours. That, at any rate, is one of the intangibilities or potentialities which give British government its peculiar character.

Rather less intangibly, the Divine Right of Kings has served to imprint on British representative government the essential dualist idea that, while government is conducted with the people's consent, it does not originate in an act of the people's will. A British Cabinet meeting is still officially 'a meeting of the Queen's confidential servants' and, as such Ministers are still recognized as having a responsibility for "the enforcement of law and order and the maintenance of an upright administration" which "no executive can share with any legislature, however answerable it may be to that legislature for the manner of its discharge".[2]

---

[1] *Eikon Basilike*, 27.
[2] Reports of Joint Select Committee on India, 1934.

N

The *authority* of government is a conception which Englishmen have, at length, agreed not to define or explicitly to locate in any single institution, but their recognition of its existence is, at least symbolically, focussed in the Crown and finds its appropriate expression in the ritual of the sovereign's Coronation.

7

With this, we complete our very summary survey of Christendom before the French Revolution. It is fashionable today to lament that the Europe which has survived the two world wars is no longer a Christian world; but that fashion of speaking is ambiguous. Certainly, it is no longer an Augustinian world; but the Augustinian world may itself have been hardly a Christian world; it may, indeed, have been Bunyan's By-Path Meadow, "the way to Doubting Castle which is kept by Giant Despair". It does not follow that our present world is no longer the world of the 'holy communion', that school in which Europe and America learnt their best practices of government. Anyway, whatever our present world has lost began to be lost, not in the middle of the twentieth century, but at the end of the eighteenth, when Hobbes' Leviathan was born in a guise of which he did not dream, the guise of Total Popular Sovereignty. We have already traced Leviathan's birth and growth in the first two sections of this study; it remains for us now to traverse the same field with a different purpose in mind: to discover what has been lost and what has survived in the history of these hundred and fifty years.

V

*The age of Leviathan 1789-1939:
Dualism and totalism*

The purpose of the last two sections of this study has been to trace the historical growth of the true alternative to Democracy: the Moral State, based upon a philosophy of Dualism. In this concluding section an attempt is made to depict this Moral State at grips with the Power State of Democracy during the one hundred and fifty years between the French Revolution and the outbreak of the Second World War, and to estimate how far it has been able to survive the pressures and the temptations of that conflict. Bearing in mind the distinction drawn in the preceding section between the two sides of the divided mind of Christendom, our conclusion is that the Augustinian Church can hardly be said to have survived at all; but that the 'holy communion', which has always been the core of the Christian Moral State, has not only survived, but has renewed itself beyond expectation. The issue remains: whether the Free World will now accept the full implications of this inheritance or whether, renouncing the responsibilities of belief, it will content itself with the devices of the Welfare State and the catchwords of national self-determination.

CHAPTER 15

The age of Leviathan: The remnants of the moral state

The French Revolution and the Old Order, 1815–1885 – Rome and London: de Maistre and the revival of mediaevalism; Castlereagh and international morality – French political thought: search for local freedoms; the Power State; the impulse towards religious revival.

I

At the end of the first chapter of this essay, we disclaimed any intention of writing the history of the 150 years from 1789 to 1939, as it should be written, in the language of high tragedy. Yet the history of that period is, inevitably, the climax of our argument, and we must, at least, attempt to indicate some of its main themes.

In our first eight chapters, we have traced in outline the growth, in this period, of the new Leviathan of popular sovereignty. In varying forms and under successive disguises, that figure dominates the scene throughout, but it does not hold the field alone.

At first sight, it might be thought that its chief adversary has been the 'Old Order' of eighteenth century monarchy – that, as Guizot wrote of France in 1820, the contest has been between "*le peuple de la Révolution*" and "*le peuple du privilège*".[1] Leviathan's prophets have always encouraged that interpretation and liberals have too commonly adopted it. Certainly, the Old Order did take up Leviathan's challenge; but it could only meet it on its own ground. To both these contestants, the State, first and last, was Power, the indivisible sovereignty of the Total People or the

---

[1] *Gouvernement de la France.* This was scarcely more than a party pamphlet, but the more significant for that.

Legitimate Monarch. In such a struggle there was no real issue, and there could be only one outcome. As candidates for total power, kings can never carry conviction; certainly not in an era of industrial revolution, and least of all to a generation like the one that came of age in the 1830's – "pantheists", as one of them recorded,

and, if not republicans, convinced that a republic is the most rational form of government and puzzled to account for the willingness of millions to persist in obedience to a single man.[1]

If Leviathan had had to meet no other opposition than this, its victory would never have been in doubt. But its real rival was a more ancient one than any parvenu Old Order; it was the dualist philosophy of the Moral State. That philosophy was equally the rival of the Old Order, and increasingly so as, in the struggle for mere power, monarchy learnt, through nationalism, the manners of totalist democracy. Dualism was still as incoherent as it had been for centuries, the more so now, perhaps, because it had to fight on these two fronts. It was uncertain of itself; it was deeply compromised, in the eyes of contemporaries, by apparent affiliations with one or other of its opponents; it wore, from time to time as many disguises as Leviathan itself, yet, in the eyes of history, it is recognizable under all of them, from the parliamentary constitutionalism of England to the re-assertion by the Roman Church of the equal sovereignty of Church and State as twin authorities, of whom

neither obeys the other within the limits to which each is restricted by its constitution.[2]

The main task of the historian of these 150 years is to trace this dualist philosophy through all its ambiguities up to the point when the collapse of the Old Order in the first World War left it to make

---

[1] Bismarck. *Gedanken und Erinnerungen.* Ch. 1.
[2] Encyclical, *Sapientiae Christianae*, 1890.

good its claim to be Leviathan's true enemy and only rational alternative.

2

We must begin with the attempt of the discredited Old Order, on the morrow of Napoleon's fall, to invest itself again with the trappings of a respectable philosophy. The prophet of that attempt was de Maistre. In his book *Du Pape*, published in 1821, he may be said to have cut down the Pope's old clothes to fit out a new race of legitimate monarchs:

There can be no human society without government, no government without sovereignty, no sovereignty without infallibility; and this last privilege is so essential that its existence must be assumed even in temporal sovereignty (where it does not reside in fact) as an essential condition of the maintenance of society.

It is, perhaps, unnecessary to comment on that statement, except to say that, for the sort of frankness which invites incredulity to the confusion of the incredulous, it has been equalled only by Hitler's *Mein Kampf*. It was a frank revival of extreme mediaeval papalism, restated in terms of the new totalism: all governments must be total, but only the Pope has the right to be total; other governments can, therefore, claim their necessary right only as a fictional reflection of his –

As the moon draws its light from the sun and is inferior to it both in quantity and quality, so royal power draws its dignity from pontifical authority.

This astonishing anachronism was not only seriously meant; it might claim to be, for Christians, on its own premise, almost logically inevitable. If Christ has delegated His own absolute sovereignty to any earthly ruler, He can have conveyed it only to the Head of His Church. As we have seen, the Augustinian Church, though often snared in this syllogism, had always, on the whole, refrained from asserting its major premise. But, in face of the Reformation schism, the Jesuit controversialists of the seventeenth century had almost, if not quite, reversed that denial; would the nineteenth century Papacy be able to persist in it in face of a far worse schism: Leviathan's new assertion of a rival absolute sovereignty? Was not Christendom now faced with an absolute choice? "It seems to me" wrote de Maistre in another work, *Considérations sur la France,*

that every true philosopher must choose between two hypotheses: either that a new religion will come to birth, or that Christianity will renew its youth in some extraordinary manner.

In such an hour of moral catastrophe, could Christians still content themselves with the belief that Christ's kingdom is not yet of this world? Was it not with a very different intention that the first act of the Pope, on his restoration in 1814, had been to give renewed recognition to the Jesuit Order, officially suppressed since 1773?

That doubt was to haunt Papal policy for more than half a century, from the day when Pius VII ceased to be Napoleon's prisoner to the day, 56 years later, when Pius IX, deprived of a temporal power which he was commonly judged to have flagrantly misused, constituted himself the 'prisoner of the Vatican'. Indeed, it was a full 70 years before the Papacy formally restated the ancient Christian doctrine of dualism:

The Almighty has divided the charge of the human race between two powers, the ecclesiastical and the civil, the one being set over divine and the other over human things. Each power is, in its kind, supreme. Each has fixed limits within which it is contained.[1]

3

That is one of the main themes of the nineteenth century. Another is the attempt to revive, in a more coherent form, the old international 'System of Europe'. It was in the discussion of this

---

[1] Encyclical *Immortale Dei*, Nov. 1, 1885.

policy that the voice of the Moral State first made itself heard in clear opposition to the Old Order.

The policy itself had been formulated by Pitt in 1805. He had then proposed to the Tsar, as the chief war aim of the Third Coalition against Napoleon, the conclusion between 'all the principal Powers of Europe' of

a treaty by which their respective rights and possessions . . . shall be fixed and recognized; and they should all bind themselves mutually to protect and support each other against any attempt to infringe them.

But, thirteen years later, when the victorious sovereigns had bound themselves to something much more ambitious, a Holy Alliance professedly based on 'the sublime truths of the religion of God our Saviour', a Cabinet of rather musty politicians in Whitehall, to whom all this was, in Castlereagh's words, "a piece of sublime mysticism and nonsense", committed themselves to something hardly less mystical:

The idea of an *Alliance Solidaire* . . . must be understood as morally implying the previous establishment of such a system of general government as may secure and enforce upon all kings and nations an internal system of peace and justice. Till the mode of constructing such a system shall have been devised . . . nothing would be more immoral or more prejudicial to the character of a government than the idea that their force should be collectively prostituted to the support of established power without any consideration of the extent to which it was abused.

This language has grown so familiar to Englishmen that they do not sufficiently realize its implications. In the context of 1818, it implied the existence of moral standards of peace and justice by which the use and abuse of political power could be more surely measured than by the Holy Allies' profession of "the sacred principles of the Christian religion". Or, of course, of any other religion; for, if Castlereagh in 1818 questioned the professions of the Holy Alliance, he questioned no less in 1821 'the loose notions of humanity and amendment' which inspired the demand for international intervention in the Greek insurrection:

I cannot be tempted or even called upon in moral duty . . . to forget the obligations of existing treaties, to endanger the form of long established relations and to aid insurrectionary efforts . . . upon the chance that it may through war mould itself into some scheme of government, but at the certainty that it must in the meantime open a field for every ardent adventurer and political fanatic in Europe.

But could statesmen who thus claimed, apparently, to be guided, in their political action, by some private moral conscience of their own, be relied on even to support consistently what Pitt had contemplated in 1805: "a general agreement and guarantee for mutual protection and security and for re-establishing a general system of public law in Europe"? Had not Castlereagh himself doubted this as early as August 1815, when he wrote:

this system of being pledged to a continental war for objects that France may any day reclaim from particular States that hold them, without pushing her demands beyond what she would contend was due to her own honour, is, I am sure, a bad British policy.

That doubt has continued to haunt British diplomacy in Europe down to our own day; but in the years after 1815 it was deepened, in European minds, by a suspicion of almost conscious hypocrisy. So much in English life and government seemed to contradict the moral pretensions of her statesmen. Was it by chance that the only two sovereigns who refused to join the Holy Alliance were Pius VII, who had just restored the Jesuits, and the Prince Regent of England, who was, in his own person, the typical representative of the characteristic English vice of that day, an arrogant misuse of unprecedented wealth – and who was, moreover, the official head of a State, preaching justice and peace, whose parliament had just passed a landlords' Corn Law and rejected the Peel-Owen Factory Bill, whose government of Ireland was becoming a European scandal, and whose Governor-

General at Calcutta was just embarking on a new campaign to establish British paramountcy in Central India?

We have suggested that Papal policy did not begin to clear itself of its ambiguities till 1885. It was, perhaps, only about the same date that British policy began to clear itself of this damning suspicion of hypocrisy. It was, at least, about that time that, after fifteen years of reforming ministries, a Conservative government extended the franchise and a Liberal Prime Minister committed himself to Irish Home Rule. One must resist the temptation to cut history into lengths, but these 70 years or so from the fall of Napoleon to the eighties of the century seem to be roughly distinguishable as an age of experiment, during which the peoples and authorities of Europe made the choices by which they had to abide in the succeeding age of power politics, world war and general revolution.

4

Between these twin ambiguities of Rome and London, a new European generation groped through these 70 years for principles of government which might save Europe both from the Old Order and from the New Leviathan. The main scene of that search was, naturally, France, for France had known both enemies at their worst and had taken their measure. As, in eighteenth century England, Whiggism became an accepted orthodoxy, against which young men and new men tended to revolt, so, in nineteenth century France, the orthodoxy of the Republic One and Indivisible became increasingly the butt of serious political thinkers. In their eyes, the Old Order was fading into ridicule; the real enemy was the Fichte-like republican mysticism preached at the Collège de France by Michelet and Quinet. And popular instinct moved in the same direction. It was intent on preserving the rights and liberties of 1789; but it was equally intent on refusing to re-embark on the adventures begun in 1792–4. The central desire of Frenchmen was still that of the *cahier* of the commune of Etampes in 1789: "how happy should we be to see feudalism destroyed". The destruction of feudalism had come, of course, to mean more than the peasant's ownership of the soil; it meant also, less tangibly but still with real force, all sorts of personal liberties and equalities; but it remains true that Frenchmen made one revolution in 1830 because they feared the resurrection of the old agrarian and clerical aristocracy, they made another in 1848 because they feared the rise of a new industrial aristocracy, and they almost welcomed the return of the Empire in 1852 because it seemed to guarantee a land-owning peasantry and bourgeois family life against the threat of proletarian socialism.

But, if the real gains of 1789 seemed thus perpetually threatened, what kind of government could make them secure? There seemed to be two possible answers; and exasperatingly enough, one seemed to lie partly in London, and the other somewhere in the direction of Rome.

The English constitution had, of course, always attracted thinking Frenchmen, from the moderates of 1789 to the Doctrinaires of the Restoration. But so long as the object of admiration was no more than what de Broglie called the 'administrative monarchy' of Whitehall and Westminster, the flirtation remained oddly platonic. Benjamin Constant did, indeed, discern in 1815 the significance of English local government as illustrating the principle that "municipal power is not a branch of the executive, but something entirely independent"; and in 1848 Lamennais retired from the constitutional committee of the National Assembly because its members refused to begin their labours by considering the organization of local government. But it was not until de Tocqueville studied English traditions in their American form that any Frenchman seemed really to understand how those traditions were rooted in the right of free association and in "the notion of private rights and the taste for local freedom", or drew the conclusion that

it is only by the struggle of collective interests, organised and pleading their own cause, that constitutional government can produce its best results.[1]

But, as de Tocqueville himself realized, freedom of association was too difficult an idea for constitutional Frenchmen; their monarchy had discouraged its practice, their republic had denied its principle. It could find a home only among the planners of a new social revolution, to whom increasingly the State itself was the real enemy and a new growth of free associations the necessary germ cells of a new society. Even to them, in spite of Constant, municipal government had become so irrevocably an organ of the central State that it could form no part of the new society. Hence, in the thirty years before Sedan, a whole series of 'group-Utopias': Fourier's *phalanges*, Blanc's *ateliers sociaux*, Proudhon's 'federative principle', Renouvier's free co-operative groups. These were not, perhaps, so Utopian as they sound, for the new groups were designed to be the representative expression of the new industrial society; and the whole confused philosophy began to come down to earth under the Third Republic in the trade union movement and in Sorel's syndicalism – till, after the war of 1914–18, it became the basis of the socialist ideology enunciated by Leon Blum in 1927:

The solution of the problem of reconstructing the State, as I seem to see it, is to split up and break down the centralised State of the classic type into a number of little technical states, based on professional organisations and functioning under the moderating authority of a central parliament, as the repository of strictly political power.[2]

---

[1] Quoted from Roger Soltau: *French Political Thought in the 19th Century;* Ernest Benn, 1931; and J. P. Mayer: *Political Thought in France;* Routledge & Kegan Paul, 1949. 'Interests' must not, of course, be understood in the pejorative modern sense. The free associations referred to were 'political, industrial, commercial and even scientific and literary'.

[2] Quoted from Soltau, *op. cit.*

Unfortunately, at the time these words were written, these Utopias were beginning to come down to earth also, and more effectively, in the Spanish *Falange,* in the Russian soviets, in Hitler's youth groups and in Mussolini's corporative State, while Marx had taken over the doctrine of the Immoral State, in which Lenin had found an argument for a new revolutionary centralization.

To an English historian, this is a pathetically futile story; but let us be clear where the pathos lies. It is the pathos of a wayfarer in a blind alley: the blind alley of the Power State. A government conceived, first and last, as an organ of power cannot decentralize; it cannot nurse life or encourage growth. It can find its justification only in war; the national unity to which it sacrifices every other social purpose is the potential unity of a nation in arms. To be able to envoke that kind of unity is always the more or less conscious calculation of the Power State, perpetually deflecting the political thought of its citizens. Bismarck, at the end of his life, confessed that he might have made a mistake in basing the federal constitution of Germany on universal suffrage. He had done so in order that, in any struggle with a coalition of foreign powers, the German Empire "might, in the last resort, have even revolutionary weapons at its command"; when he came to doubt whether he had not overrated the German voters' sense of national unity, he comforted himself with the hope that

in times of war, national feeling will always rise high enough to tear away the web of lies in which sectional leaders, ambitious orators and party newspapers keep the masses entangled in times of peace.[1]

The attachment of Frenchmen to a highly centralized form of government has been determined by the same calculation. From 1830 until today, war has been their constant underlying assumption – at first from love of it, then from idealization of it, and, in

---

[1] *Gedanken und Erinnerungen* Chs. 21 and 33.

the end, from fear of it.[1] To them, local or group freedoms have always implied pacifism; they have never believed, what better balanced governments have proved to be true, that such freedoms may be the best climate for national unity, even in war – a mild climate, actually more favourable to the growth of a powerful central executive than the strong suns and storms of a sovereign parliament.

They have often justified their scepticism by a sort of historic fatalism. *"L'histoire suit sa pente";* it is too late to put the clock back. Yet, historically, centralization has a no more ancient tradition in France than in England or Holland, and has been no more inevitable. In the middle of the eighteenth century, Montesquieu was looking back for no more than 150 years when he wrote:

Formerly, every French village was a capital: today, there is only one great capital. Every part of the State used to be a centre of power; today, everything depends on the Centre, and the Centre has become, in effect, the whole State.

And the men of 1789 did actually put back the clock. The French constitution of 1791 need not have failed any more than the Canadian constitution of the same year, if its communal units had been reasonably linked with a constitutional monarchy. What is true is that local freedoms in France had long lost the non-political roots from which, as we have suggested, they drew their essential strength in England and America. A bad fiscal system had left no room for local enterprise and had stifled the indepen-

---

[1] E.g. Louis Blanc in the 1840s: "to spread out, to overflow, is a duty. What France fails to get in heroic adventures, she will get in popular risings". (Quoted from Soltau. *op. cit.*) Napoleon III in the 1850s: "a government can safely break the law, and even suppress liberty, but it will soon perish if it does not take the lead in the great causes of civilization". And Hanotaux, ex-Foreign Minister in 1913: "the French people have in their very veins this idea of unity through power. In time of danger they fear nothing so much as dismemberment." (*La France en 1614*).

dence of trade guilds and municipalities. Local freedoms had become privileges, granted, and periodically renewed, by the king for value received. The elected syndics of the communes had been caught up into the administrative machine of the royal Intendants.

5

Above all, French freedoms lacked the religious roots which might have nourished in them the faculty of independent moral judgement. By a tragic accident, 300 years before the Reformation, France had learnt, in the extraordinary circumstances of the Albigensian crusade, the habit of levying war against anomalous religious dissent. The methods she then learnt she applied in turn to Waldenses, Calvinists and Jansenists. The main crisis of her Reformation took the form of a civil war, partly between rival aristocracies, partly between two foreign patriarchates centralized at Rome and Geneva. In the established Gallican Church of the eighteenth century, bishops, with a few notorious exceptions, were at least as respectable as in England and the parish clergy were much more of one class and mind with their people; but, in the diocese, the hierarchy formed, all too consciously, a separate secular Estate, with its own interests and its own privileges, while, in the parish, the *curé* was almost as much the agent of a central system of ecclesiastical administration as the syndics of a secular. His one root of independence was in a security of tenure comparable with the English 'parson's freehold', and that root was cut by Napoleon's re-organization.

In spite of her anti-clericalism, the France of the 1830s was, perhaps more conscious of this religious poverty than of the mere over-centralization of her government. Even Quinet, the republican mystic, regretted that the men of 1789 had stopped short of real religious revolution, and had thus missed the opportunity of giving to democracy a solid moral basis in some sort of Unitarian

Church. A little later, even Comte, the would-be prophet of a strictly 'scientific' philosophy of government, could not resist the temptation to invent a religion to fit it. Much more, Guizot, the Protestant politician, regretted that the defenders of constitutional monarchy had no religious impulse to set against 'revolutionary fanaticism'. "Our weakness", he said in 1832,

is that our political and moral convictions are uncertain. . . . Even without political power, religion is a social principle, the natural ally and necessary support of all regular government. It gives to all government an elevation of character and a greatness which otherwise it too often lacks. . . . Humanity cannot for long dispense with greatness.[1]

That last phrase – *l'humanité ne se passe pas longtemps de grandeur* – deserves to live as the epitaph of innumerable parliamentary governments, not least of Guizot's own; but, for the rest, these calculations of political utility were, of course, beside the point. Religion is, no doubt, a 'social principle', but only if it begins by being something more. A State religion cannot be, as such, a witness to truth. God must be worshipped for His own sake, not for the sake of His social utility. To forget this in their search for a compelling *unité morale* has been, perhaps, the besetting sin of French political thinkers – and, indeed, of all 'democratic' thought in Europe. An English liberal summed up that error in writing of Cavour in 1861:

The theory of liberty insists on the independence of the Church; the theory of liberalism insists on the omnipotence of the State as the organ of the popular will.[2]

In France, at any rate, clear thinking about the essential dualism of Church and State has been curiously rare. It may be the more worth while to quote, from the French parliamentary debates of the 1820s, one statement of the principle:

---

[1] Quoted from Thureau-Dangin. *La Monarchie de Juillet.*
[2] Acton. *Historical Essays and Studies.* Macmillan, 1908.

Human societies are born, live and die on the earth; there they fulfil their destinies; there ends their imperfect and faulty justice whose only foundation is their need and right of self-preservation. But man in his entirety is not bounded by them. When men commit themselves to society, they keep back the best part of themselves, those high faculties by which they rise to God. . . . I know that it is in the interest of governments to ally themselves with religion. . . . But this alliance can never include more than the visible externals of religion, its worship and the place of its ministers in the State. Truth can have no part in it; for truth does not belong to the domain of power, nor depend upon the protection of men.[1]

These words of Royer-Collard, the Jansenist independent, fall far short of the whole truth, but, when they were spoken, they came nearer than more official pronouncements, ecclesiastical or political, to express the feelings of a younger generation of Frenchmen who had grown up under the shadow of the closing years of Napoleon's rule. It was not only ineffectual romanticists of that generation, like de Musset who asked helplessly:

And what is left to us, to us the deicides?

A much more sober representative of that generation wrote later of the France of his youth:

What did one think in those days? Did one trouble to think? . . . What great idea did not seem an absurdity? We had come to the end of everything, of glory no less than liberty. Politics had no principles. Morality had been gradually reduced to the practice of useful virtues; it was valued as a condition of order, not as a source of dignity. Religion was accepted as a political necessity, but controversy, enthusiasm and proselytism were alike forbidden to it. It seemed useless to discuss it and unseemly to defend it. . . . Reason itself was, one might say, humiliated by the disappointment of its hopes and exhausted by its adventures. Someone asked M. Sieyes: 'what do you think'? – 'I do not think', he replied, and he spoke for everyone. The mind of man has seldom taken less pride in itself than in those days.[2]

---

[1] Spuller, *op. cit.*
[2] Remusat, quoted from Spuller, *op. cit.*

This last sentence may seem strange to us who have come to think of the nineteenth century as the age of man's intellectual triumph over nature. This generation stood, after all, well over the threshold of that age. Lavoisier had been in his grave only twenty years; Lamark and Cuvier were still at work. Yet, in fact, science, as we understand it, hardly came to impress itself on the public mind of France – or, indeed of Europe – until after the publication of the *Origin of Species* in 1859. To the generation of whom we are speaking, 'science' meant the social speculations of the encyclopaedists which had been discredited by the failures of the Revolution. Even in the England of those days, the England of Dalton and Davy, experimental science was to remain modestly tentative throughout the first half of the century, content to declare its results from no more imposing platform than the lecture theatre of Faraday's Royal Institution. Technology was already winning its first triumphs in England, though hardly yet in France – but what triumphs! If the French Revolution had discredited the 'science' of d'Alembert and Condorcet in terms of human progress, the industrial revolution was no less discrediting the 'science' of Cartwright and Watt in terms of mere decent human feeling.

No, the disillusionment of those days was real, and was not peculiar to France. Science did not yet even claim to provide an answer to it. Even Englishmen were becoming conscious that their ingrained political moralities, which Continental statesmen found so incomprehensible and so irritating, needed some better authority than a tradition of duty inherited from a more vivid religious past. Hence the impulse towards a religious revival which France shared, at that time, with all Europe. That is, perhaps, the most dominant theme of the nineteenth century; it is certainly the most tragic of its themes.

CHAPTER 16

The age of Leviathan: The Christian revival

The idea of a Universal Church: abortive revivals of the early nineteenth century; emergence of new prospects before 1914 – The Anglican Missionary Church – The Roman Teaching Church.

I

The picture of European thought in the seventy years after Waterloo, which we have sketched in the last chapter, has been one of ambiguity and failure; and we have suggested that it is fundamentally the picture of an anaemic society waiting for the blood transfusion of a religious revival. That revival came. Though its history during these same seventy years seems hardly less a history of ambiguity and failure, it had developed thirty years later, on the eve of the first world war, at least some of the necessary conditions for a re-animation of the Christian Moral State. That is the theme of this chapter.

But, in writing of religious revival, it is necessary to remind ourselves again that we are writing the history of the State, not of the Church – or, at any rate, of the Church only from the point of view of the State. Within these limits, a historian cannot deal adequately with religious movements which, by their very nature, transcend all considerations of political organization. We can deal only with those movements whose effect upon the State can be clearly traced. There were, doubtless, other movements in the Christian Church which have not yet exerted a visible influence outside the 'holy communion' of the Church itself; and some of these may even prove, in the long run, to have been more important to the cultural, and even the political, future of Europe. But these are beyond the scope of a historian who does not wish to venture upon prophecy.

2

Macaulay, reviewing Ranke's History of the Popes in 1840, drew attention to "the progress of the Catholic revival of the 19th century" as to an already accomplished and "singularly interesting" fact. He was referring only to "the unchangeable Church" of Rome, whose "power over the thoughts and minds of men", he said, "is now greater far than it was when the Encyclopaedia and the Philosophical Dictionary appeared"; and he wondered why, in contrast,

neither the moral revolution of the 18th century, nor the moral counter-revolution of the 19th, should have, in any perceptible degree, added to the domain of Protestantism.

In this he perhaps missed a point. His words "Catholic revival" might have been applied, with almost equal truth, to the contemporary movement of Christian thought outside the Roman Church. Even in its most Protestant forms, it was a catholic movement. It was a revival of the perennial idea of the 'holy communion'; but, almost for the first time in the history of Christendom, the revival did not take the form of monastic withdrawal or of sectarian separatism, except as a refuge after failure. Its central appeal was to the Church as a whole; its central aspiration was, at its weakest, towards what Thomas Arnold called "a truly national and Christian Church" and, at its strongest, in the words of F. D. Maurice, towards "a Church Universal, founded upon the very nature of God Himself".[1] To the Anglican, the Free Churchman and the Lutheran, such a Church had to be re-discovered; to the Roman Catholic it was already 'given', but it had still to be liberated from its entanglements with the Old

---

[1] Quoted from Basil Willey, *Nineteenth Century Studies,* Chatto and Windus, 1949.

Order, from (to use Lacordaire's phrase) "the fatal alliance between throne and altar".

The tone in which one writes of this movement will depend on one's time scale. On any time scale, it must be something of a tragedy, but the quality of the tragedy will be different. If the time scale be the life of Macaulay's generation, of whom Melbourne said ruefully in 1839 that "all the young men are gone mad upon religion" – let us say, the generation born in the first decade of the century, with a few of their elders – the story can hardly be written except as an almost unrelieved personal tragedy. In England, it is the tragedy of Newman and Maurice, and of that earlier figure, Edward Irving, whose memory has recently begun to re-emerge from a kind of fantastic obscurity. In France, it is the tragedy of Lamennais, Lacordaire and Montalembert, and of the whole Liberal Catholic movement. In Italy, it may almost be said to be the tragedy of Pius IX himself in the first years of his pontificate, 1846–49. In Germany, Döllinger's tragedy belongs to a rather later chapter of the story, but there is a minor tragedy in the fate of the diplomatist, Bunsen, an older friend of Melbourne's 'young men', who deserves at least to be remembered for his description of the disillusionment of those whose hopes had been centred in the national aspects of the revival. In 1838 Bunsen had greeted Gladstone's *The State in its relations with the Church* with the significant confession: "his Church is my Church, the divine consciousness of the State"; in 1854 he wrote:

The old order of things is judged; forty years of peace have not improved it. I have bidden adieu to politics . . . and, in Church matters, I have spoken the word by which I hope to abide and in which I hope to die: I go from the Jews to the Gentiles, from the Church to the congregation, and I leave the dead to bury their dead.[1]

"From the Church to the congregation" seems a good enough sign-post to Lacordaire's journey from the pulpit of Notre Dame

---

[1] Bunsen. Memoirs.

to his Dominican cloister, and of Maurice's and Döllinger's from their University chairs to a Working Men's College or an Old Catholic sect.

If, however, we extend our time scale to the first years of the twentieth century, the eve of the first world war, the story is still a tragedy, and a more public one, but it is a tragedy relieved by at least a glimpse of farther horizons.

On that scale (to speak first of the tragedy) the story of close on a hundred years begins, it would seem, in a clear challenge to Leviathan; in a revolt against worldliness, a renunciation of political alliances, a revived belief in the operation of the Holy Spirit in a Universal Church, a renewed recognition of that Church as the sphere in which God has chosen to work out His scheme of human salvation. It seems to end in an identification between Christianity and political action more complete and systematic, perhaps, than had been asserted at any earlier period in the history of Christendom. In Germany, this secularization of religious thought, avowed by Wellhausen in the words we have already quoted,[1] seemed to confirm the Lutheran Church in completer servility to the State. But the avowal was not peculiar to Germany; a French Calvinist echoed it in 1903:

The kingdom of God comes through the State. . . . We are theocrats. . . . Let the wiseacres condemn our madness in the name of the monstrous distinction between Church and State. It is on earth that we desire to see our heavenly country, a holy system of politics.[2]

In England, such secularization was, as usual, not much more than a climate of opinion, that social-ist climate which we have tried to describe in earlier chapters. What is ominously significant is that, at the beginning of the twentieth century, it was the stormy climate of the Education controversy, a political battle, waged between the Established and Free Churches with purely political

---

[1] Page 82.
[2] Quoted from Paul Seippel, *Les Deux Frances*, 1905, pp. 392–3.

weapons in a temper of political bitterness. In Catholic Europe, the Papacy had been driven by the Italian revolution more deeply than ever into dependence on the thrones of the Old Order. In attempting to re-assert its independence after 1878, Leo XIII had failed to carry with him the French Catholics on whom, for more than twenty years, his predecessor had relied for the defence of his temporal power; and the Church in France was struggling in the political mire of the Dreyfus case, the Combes legislation and the propaganda of the *Action Française*. Meanwhile, Leviathan seemed to have been reborn in the respectable guise of nationalism and was gathering its forces for the catastrophe of 1914, unrestrained and unguided by any authoritative witness to eternal truth. In 1914, indeed, Englishmen might well look back on a prophecy which Charles Kingsley had ventured 65 years before, towards the close of the Christian Socialist phase of the English revival:

We are entering fast, I both hope and fear, into the region of prodigy, true and false; and our great-grandchildren will look back on the latter half of this century and ask if it were possible that such things could happen in an organised planet.[1]

The prophecy was a little antedated, but by the end of this story had it not come true?

Yet, by the end (to speak now of horizons beyond the tragedy) there were at least two prodigies which were not wholly prodigies of confusion and disaster. Through the storm-clouds of politics there were emerging, in England, a missionary Church and, in Rome, a teaching Church.

3

The construction of a 'second British Empire' after the American Revolution is, on the whole, less astonishing than the transformation of the insular Church of England of the early

---

[1] Epilogue of *Yeast*, 1849.

nineteenth century into the world patriarchate of the early twentieth.

Indeed, the transformation was more sudden that this. It was accomplished in hardly more than fifty years, for it consisted, not simply in an intensification of missionary enterprise, but in the creation of a missionary Church. The Establishment in England had acquired in the eighteenth century the bad habit of leaving the pioneer preaching of the gospel to missionary societies, which it supported but could not integrate into itself. It was bound, itself, to a legal status which confined it to its island home; if it emigrated, it could do so only as a State Church, and, as such, its appearance overseas might have dangerous political implications. So, when the first British Empire was lost, the North American continent was still no more than an anomalous appendage of the diocese of London; Lambeth sent its first overseas bishop to India in 1814, enjoining him to 'avoid enthusiasm', with the implication that enthusiasm should be left to the societies; Upper Canada had to wait for its first Anglican bishop until 1839, nearly half a century after the constitution of 1791.[1] In significant contrast, the 'saddle-bag preachers' of Methodism appeared among the congregations of American colonial Christianity, not as the pioneers of a new dissenting sect, but as the apostles of a Church – almost of *the* Church, and, by the necessities of their task, an episcopal Church at that.

It was long before the Establishment found a way to follow this example. The formative years of the 'second empire' in Australasia and Africa were dominated by the missionary societies, and their influence on British colonial policy was as doubtful as the influence of the friars on mediaeval Christendom in its decline, or of the Jesuits on the policies of the Counter-Reformation. A Church cannot with impunity delegate the preaching of the

---

[1] The Anglican diocese of Quebec, which dates from 1793, was an isolated anomaly.

gospel to semi-independent auxiliaries. One result, especially under a parliamentary system of government, is that such auxiliaries so easily become political pressure groups, agitating for measures less far-sighted than statesmanship would suggest and narrower than can be justified by Christian doctrine. Much of the confused tragedy of race relations in South Africa today can be traced back to the half-truths and snap judgements of the years which immediately followed the abolition of slavery. It was hardly until the middle of the century, in the days of Bishop Selwyn in the South Pacific and Archbishop Gray at the Cape, that the English Establishment began to transcend the secular law of its being and to find its spiritual place at the centre of a world communion of Churches.

It would hardly have made that discovery if it had not made another nearer home. It would not have become something like a Universal Church if it had not become, in more than the legal sense, a national Church, concerned with what a later Pope was to call a "mission within the fold". At home, too, it learnt late. It had missed the opportunity of evangelism in the eighteenth century when Wesley had seized it; and, again, nearly half the next century had elapsed before it came to realize the dereliction of the new people of England which the industrial revolution had brought into being in the fifty hectic years since Wesley's death.

In the interval, the character of the problem had changed. Wesley had had to preach mainly to ignorance and social isolation. Except in the 'hovels'[1] of the new mining settlements, physical conditions of life were, perhaps, hardly worse than they had been for centuries, though the ancient town and village economies were beginning, as it were, to burst at their seams under the pressure of a swelling population and the process of rural enclo-

---

[1] The technical word in common use on the Tyne at the beginning of the eighteenth century.

sure.[1] But now to the neglects of that earlier period were added the almost deliberate crimes of the Steam Age: a wholesale concentration of population; a shoddy urban development, reckless of sanitation and decency; low wages, the sweat-shop and child labour. Under these conditions, the way towards a spiritually effective national Church led necessarily through the slums; and, in that Valley of Humiliation, the 'faith once delivered to the saints' tended to translate itself into a 'social gospel', which was, in large part, a political programme. To the Christian Socialist of the 'forties it was a programme of sanitary reform; to the East End missions of the 'eighties it was a programme of support for the dockers in their struggle for better wages; to the young men of the first years of the twentieth century it was the heterogeneous programme of English social-ism. That was one of the impulses which gave to the generation born in the eighteen-forties "the exhilarating sense of being upon a rising tide".[2]

On the whole, the wonder is that the political programme did not submerge the faith. There are no clearly definable bounds between Church and State; Christian dualism does not consist in the delimitation of fixed frontiers. The Christian call to an utter 'change of mind' must always be, in some measure, a call to change laws which embody an old mind – the more so since law, by embodying an old mind, tends to raise its 'corrupt affections' to something like the dignity of Rousseau's "compulsory sentiments of sociability". Such a call may well seem imperative for an official Church in a State where the Christian

---

[1] The worst evils of the industrial revolution of which Adam Smith was conscious in 1776 were the depressing intellectual effect on the industrial worker of "the progress of the division of labour", and the moral effect on a "man of low condition" of removal from village to town. "While he remains in a country village, his conduct may be attended to and he may be obliged to attend to it himself. . . . But as soon as he comes into a great city, he is sunk in obscurity. . . . He never emerges so effectually from this obscurity . . . , as by his becoming the member of a small religious sect."

[2] Bishop E. S. Talbot. *Memories of Early Life.* 1924.

communicant is also a parliamentary voter, and at times when the dominant political philosophy explicitly declares "the pursuit of an enlightened self-interest" to be, not only a civic right, but almost a civic duty. The frontier is crossed only when the call ceases to be addressed to the individual conscience, when the end aimed at is no longer a change in individual minds but a change in a social balance of power, and when the means used is a mobilization of new self-interests to counteract old ones – in a word, when the call becomes a crusade. The Augustinian Church militant is never far from that frontier and was never, perhaps, more prone to crusade across it than in the contemporary Europe of Bismarck and Pius IX.

If, in these years, the frontier was so little crossed by the home missionaries of the Church in England, it was because their social-ist temper was only one of the two impulses which had launched them on the 'rising tide', and much the less powerful of the two. More powerful was the impulse of the so-called Oxford Movement. That movement had begun (so Newman afterwards reckoned) in Keble's Assize sermon on 'National Apostasy' in 1833; and, in all its subsequent phases, it conceived the Church's mission to be rather the re-conversion of an apostate State than the reform of an unjust one. The agent of that re-conversion was to be an independent Church far removed from the calculations and judgements of men. "They think", wrote Newman to the clergy of the Church in this same year, speaking of the political reformers of the day,

They think that they have given and can take away. They have been deluded into a notion that present palpable usefulness, produceable results, acceptableness to your flocks, that these and such like are the tests of your divine commission. Enlighten them in this matter. Magnify your office. If you have the Spirit of the apostles on you, stir up the gift of God which is in you.

Polemics never express the real spirit of any movement; certainly

Newman's indignation did not express the temper of that great central body of piety which drew so much of its inspiration from Oxford and was to be so largely responsible for giving the Church of England its direction over the next two generations. Still, though that body was to take over the 'social gospel' from the Christian Socialists with a new enthusiasm, it never lost the sense of the Church as an independent authority in its own right, whose words and acts could not be measured by standards of political prudence or social utility.

This is not the portrait of an ideal Church. An ideal Church would not have entangled itself in the polemics about education and Welsh disestablishment in the decade before 1914; nor would it, perhaps, have been so prone, after 1918, to mistake democracy for Christian brotherhood and the League of Nations for the Kingdom of God. But it did, comparatively speaking, achieve something like a real pattern of Christian dualism. And in political philosophy and practice, imperfect patterns are better than even perfect ideals, for they can be copied. There was nothing about the English pattern so recondite as to preclude its imitation by other nations. Its simple secret was that in Great Britain the dilemma between the Old Order and the Revolution never presented itself in the same pseudo-logical form as on the continent of Europe, as a conflict between Church and State. Here, in 1914 as in 1815, Church and State seemed to remain committed to an alliance which neither the bitterest Free Church critics of the English establishment, nor the Free Kirk seceders in Scotland, nor the advocates of a scientific agnosticism, really desired to break. Here alone, in spite of some gross anomalies, a free Christian Church could exist in a free Christian State: a Church spiritually free, but claiming no secular immunities, could bring its blessing to a State free from the threat of ecclesiastical censures, but admitting, on the whole, the authority of the Church to set a standard for men's thoughts and a goal for their desires. Here alone, a constitutional monarchy upheld the truth of government by consent, while barring, by its very existence, the heresies of popular sovereignty. Here alone, the Christian social reformers of the revival, like Shaftesbury, though they must, after Wilberforce's example, renounce ordinary political ambition, could hope to see their ideals triumph against both conservative reaction and socialist revolution. They ran, at least, no risk of the fate that overtook Ozanam's Society of St Vincent de Paul in France in the latter years of the Second Empire: suppression by a suspicious police State. Here alone, therefore, the Christian politician, conservative or radical, could serve both Church and State with no more – though no less – sense of tension than the Christian grocer or the Christian works manager. In all this, there was, no doubt, much Laodicean muddle-headedness, much of what it is now the fashion to deprecate as 'diffused Christianity', too much of the gentleman's or the trade unionist's code and too little of faith and worship, too much of policy and too little of doctrine; but there was at least more faith and worship in the Westminster of Gladstone and Salisbury than in that of Castlereagh and Melbourne, and more doctrine in the Lambeth of Davidson than in that of Sutton or of Sumner.

4

If the emergence of this pattern in England, with all its defects, will thus seem something of a prodigy to a future historian who can survey the Age of Leviathan dispassionately from a distance, he will be even more struck by the change which began to come over the 'unchangeable Church' of Rome in the thirty years before 1914. He will probably, indeed, be kinder to the 'reactionary' Popes of the previous seventy years than were the Liberal historians of the early twentieth century and he will be careful not to contrast them too sharply with their successors; but, on the other hand, he will be able to see in Leo XIII and Pius X, not so

much the successors of Gregory XVI and Pius IX, as the pre-
cessors of Pius XI and Pius XII in the years between the wars.
That lengthened perspective will make all the difference to the
story. For, while the new English pattern was already plain
enough in 1914, needing only to be completed by a working
reconciliation between the Established and Free Churches, the
new Roman pattern hardly became distinct until it was thrown
into relief against the darkening background of European totalism
in the days of Mussolini and Hitler.

The first reaction of the Papacy to the French revolution had
not been one of unmixed hostility. Pius VI hesitated long before
he condemned the Civil Constitution of the clergy. His successor, Pius VII, had already attracted Napoleon's attention by a
Christmas sermon in 1797, in which he almost welcomed the
French armies in Northern and central Italy:

The democratic rule now introduced among us is not opposed to the
gospel: it demands, on the contrary, the lofty virtues that are only to be
attained in the school of Jesus Christ.[1]

When he became Pope, the formal reconciliation of revolutionary
France to the Church seemed to him worth all the compromises
of the Concordat of 1801 and all the humiliations of Napoleon's
coronation in 1805 – worth, too, endurance of all the treacheries
which, under cover of the Concordat, created the *église caserne*,
the barrackroom Church of the Empire. Though the experiment
ended in his own deposition and imprisonment, he never regretted
it, nor ceased to be grateful to Napoleon for having made it
possible.

Conceivably, after his death in 1823, his successors might have
inherited his instinct for reconciliation and might have acted on
it more effectively, if they had been only the spiritual heads of a
Universal Church, unburdened by a temporal sovereignty. So,
at least, a non-Catholic historian must think. As it was, their

---

[1] Quoted from Nielsen, *History of the Papacy in the Nineteenth Century*.

teaching about Christian principles of government was coloured by the politics of Italy and discredited by the abuses of their own administration. Already in 1821 Rome had had to welcome as allies an Austrian army advancing on revolutionary Naples; in 1830 and 1832 Gregory XVI had to invite a similar invasion to restore order in Romagna itself. When in 1846 Pius IX succeeded as a 'liberal' Pope and, as such, a possible President of a federated Italy, he found it was no longer enough to clear his political reputation by renouncing the patronage of Austria; he was required to deny his spiritual status by declaring war on her. Restored to a diminished sovereignty after the interlude of the Roman Republic and Cavour's occupation of central Italy, he found himself the client, no longer of Austria, but of France. Could there be a clearer demonstration that, for the Head of the Church, temporal power was, at least in nineteenth century Europe, no guarantee of spiritual independence, but a badge of political servitude?

In these entanglements, the Papacy could not ignore the challenge of Leviathan, but could venture no answer to it save the mere denials of the Old Order. The real vice of Gregory XVI's encyclical *Mirari Vos* in 1832 and of Pius IX's *Syllabus of Errors* in 1864 was, not so much that they were unsound within their limits, as that they were purely negative. There is nothing more tempting to conservatives than to 'debunk' the new catchwords of the hour; but it is a temptation beneath the dignity of a chief pastor. He cannot feed his flock by crying 'wolf', even when the wolf is at the door. Thus, to us who know the history of Leviathan, the condemnation in *Mirari Vos* of the "absurd and erroneous maxim that liberty of conscience must be granted to all" seems hardly more injudicious than Montalembert's assertion, to which it was, in some sort, a reply, that "the Church can venture without fear or distrust on the vast ocean of democracy"; but, even by debating standards, it was an inadequate reply. Still more, the condemnation by the *Syllabus* of the proposition that "the Roman Pontiff can and must effect a reconciliation and alliance with progress, liberty and the new civilisation" may well seem to us no more than a platitude, for, if eternal truth has been, in any measure, revealed to man, it obviously cannot be accommodated to the changing fashions of political thought, least of all to fashions so ambiguous as those of popular sovereignty; but the condemnation deserved the remonstrance of the Archbishop of Paris:

Thy reproof is mighty, thou Vicar of Christ, but thy blessing is mightier still. God has set thee between the two halves of this century, in order to close the one and to inaugurate the other. Thou art he who shall defend reason and faith, liberty and authority, politics and the Church.[1]

Yet, if in these years Rome missed the mark, there was a mark to be hit. Most political 'rights' are, in their origin, not claims to be right, but claims to be let alone. The law of England leaves Englishmen free to practise the religion of their choice, but it still commissions the Established Church to pray for deliverance from the sin of 'will-worship'. The common sense of mankind has come to the conclusion that governments cannot safely be trusted to limit freedom of speech or to license printing; but it recognizes, none the less, that unbridled controversy is a serious moral evil. It has been the favourite trick of Leviathan to break down social order by converting all such negative limits to the compulsion of law into positive moral principles – and then to deny even the negative limits when it comes to build up a new social order of its own. The spiritual head of Christendom might well think it his urgent duty to expose this trick of 'self-determination', the more so because it is a trick which can be played successfully even on honest liberals of the English and American type. For instance, in America, Justice Holmes' famous dissenting judgement in the Abrams case in 1919 may be thought to come dangerously near the line where the negative principle of the American Constitution,

---

[1] Nielsen, *op. cit.*

P

that "Congress shall make no law . . . abridging the freedom of speech", is converted into a positive doctrine of very dubious value – the doctrine "that the best test of truth is the power of thought to get itself accepted in the market". Certainly, there was a real danger lest, in 1832, the Liberal Catholics of France might fall victims to the trick. They meant by their formula of a 'free Church in a free State' no more than that, under a free government like that of England, the Church need claim no other legal liberties than those enjoyed by all associations alike; but, as events were to prove, the formula could as easily be made to mean the primitive dualism of divorce between the State and the Moral Law; it might mean the existence of a hermit Church in an irreligious State. Moreover, in international affairs, these liberal Catholics, inconsistently enough, were in danger of inflating the revolutionary enthusiasms of the Paris mob into the fervours of a crusade – a crusade for the political 'liberation' of Catholic populations in Ireland and Poland. A Papacy confronted by Mazzini could not be expected to encourage the hero-worship of O'Connell, nor to appreciate the beauties of English parliamentary government when faced with the anti-clerical legislation of Anglophil statesmen in Piedmont.

5

What might have been expected of it, if it had not been preoccupied with the politics of Italy, was that it should discern that there were other spirits of change at work in Christendom than those of nationalism and anti-clericalism, and other spirits of conservation than those of the Old Order. Already in 1832, and still more in 1864, the idea of a parliamentary State, distinctively Catholic, yet none the less based on toleration and freedom of association, was something more than a debatable dream; it was actually being realized in Belgium. To the future historian, the oddest failure of Rome in the mid-nineteenth century will surely seem to be that it ignored the emergence of a new Catholic State which, in the next century, was to become the natural home of the premier Catholic University of Europe. Indeed, such a historian may be tempted to describe the change that began to come over the Vatican in the last twenty years of the century by saying that Leo XIII learnt to look at politics with Belgian, instead of with Italian, or even French, eyes; he may even be tempted to add that the change was not accomplished until, between the wars of the next century, Pius XI and Pius XII, finding themselves responsible for vast Catholic populations in the United States, could begin to look at politics with American, rather than with European, eyes.

He is, however, even more likely to describe the change as a withdrawal from all political points of vantage or dispute, back to an altogether stronger level of argument: to the primitive Christian argument for a Change of Mind. He will find that argument emerging more and more clearly from the Papal pronouncements of sixty years, until it culminates in the appeal of 1939:

Was there ever an age which suffered more from mental starvation, from a deeply rooted impoverishment of the human soul? It has surely fulfilled the prophecy of the Apocalypse: 'thou has said, I am rich and increased with goods and have need of nothing, and knowest not that thou art wretched and miserable and poor and blind and naked'. . . . A renewal of men's minds, proportioned to the changed circumstances and needs of the hour, is the task of the Catholic Church.[1]

In the light of that argument he may be less impressed by the imposing succession of encyclicals in which Leo XIII, the canon jurist, redefined the Church's teaching on the nature and functions of the State and the principles of social justice, than by the reforms of Church worship and order associated with the name of Pius X, and by the educational revival launched by Pius XI. He will not,

---

[1] Encyclical *Summi Pontificatus* October 20, 1939.

indeed, make the mistake of supposing that this later Papacy in any degree abandoned its claims to universal authority. He will note the recurrence of such assertions as

the deposit of truth entrusted to Us by God and Our weighty office of declaring . . . the entire moral law demand that both the social order and economic life be brought within Our supreme jurisdiction.[1]

But he will note also the interpretation put upon this 'jurisdiction'. He may well draw the astonishing picture of a Papacy, newly armed in 1870 with all the thunders of infallibility, choosing increasingly to speak to peoples rather than to governments, to assert the simplest truths rather than to confute heresies, to rebuke the commonest sins rather than to rebut governmental infringements of the rights of the Church, to rouse the laity to their social duties rather than to vindicate the authority of the priesthood, and, when asserting Christian rights in the world of politics, to concentrate almost exclusively on the sanctity of the family and on the right of parents to control their children's education. It is as though the Church had chosen at last to take Leviathan at its word and, since there is no sovereign but the people, to convince that sovereign that there is no other source of social evil, nor hope of social amendment, than in its own beliefs and standards of conduct.

In 1861 Lord Acton had suggested that the Church of Rome would be able to dispense with temporal power only

in a State in which rights are sacred, in which the independence of the two orders is a fundamental and essential principle, in which property is secured, and in which government usurps no social functions.[2]

Yet, in fact, it seems to have relearnt its primitive language of spiritual authority only, seventy years later, as a persecuted Church in a totalist world order, where States admitted no such

---

[1] Encyclical *Quadragesimo Anno* May 15, 1931.
[2] *Cavour, loc. cit.*

principle, and recognized no limits to their social omnipotence. In that context, even its faltering language of 'natural law' regained something of its primitive force, as thus, in challenge to Nazi Germany:

The believer has an inalienable right to profess his faith and put it into practice in the manner suited to him. Laws that suppress or make this profession and practice difficult contradict the natural law. . . . Parents have a primary and original right to determine the education of the children given them by God in the spirit of the true faith. . . . Laws . . . that disregard the rights of parents guaranteed to them by natural law . . . are utterly and essentially immoral.[1]

Time assuredly has its revenges. Addressing the republicans of France shortly after the revolution of 1848, a bishop of Orleans, discountenanced by Rome, had claimed that French Catholics could accept whole-heartedly the principles inherent in

the spirit of the French Revolution . . . free institutions, liberty of conscience, political liberty, civil and individual liberty, the liberty of families, freedom of education, liberty of opinion.[2]

The course of history was to show that he fundamentally misconceived the spirit of the Revolution, but not fundamentally the spirit of the Roman Church or the nature of the moral law to which, in the last resort, the Church itself was to appeal against the laws of totalist power.

---

[1] Encyclical *Mit Brennender Sorge* March 14, 1937.
[2] Montalembert: *Mémoire de l'Abbé Loeordaire*, 1863.

CHAPTER 17

The free world

Christianity since 1914 – Restatement of Christian dualism – The assets of
the Free World – Colonial expansion and the colour bar – Freedom and the
Welfare State.

I

The picture we have tried to draw in our later chapters is of
some surviving seedlings of dualism, already half choked
by the confused growths of post-mediaeval Christendom,
struggling to re-establish themselves in the parching climate of
democratic totalism. For the most part, though not entirely, this
picture has been of the Europe of 1914. We shall not try to bring
it up to date, for the last thirty or forty years are not yet in focus,
at any rate to one who has lived through them. Nor can we widen
our canvas to take in the American continent, for that would
require a separate study. But one thing at least is clear: that the
survivals of 1914 have since grown stronger in the patches of soil
where they had taken root and have even spread to other soils.
To a cursory observer, they still do not make much show, and
their hold is all too precarious; but they have responded to cultivation and, still more, they have thriven on adversity.

About the influence of adversity, at any rate, there can be no
doubt. In Europe, the years since 1914 began by destroying the
State systems which represented, in one form or another, the
subjection of Church to State or of State to Church: the State-
Church of the Tsars, the Church-State of the Hapsburgs, the
domestic-chaplain-Church of the Hohenzollerns. Since that
beginning, these years have forced upon almost every branch of
the Church in Europe the experience of living under State systems

with which no Christian alliance is possible: in Russia, Germany and Italy between the wars, in the occupied countries of Northern Europe from 1940 to 1945, and today in East Germany and in all the territories behind the 'iron curtain'. That experience has brought home to European Christians, as never before, the precarious tenure of the Augustinian Church as an authority, sharing the responsibilities of world government, and, by contrast, the strength of the older idea of the Church as an independent society, with its own life and its own mission.

Of course, no such experience is, in itself, pure gain. A Church so schooled in resistance to oppression, remembers that it is a Church of the people, rather than of rulers; and, whenever it regains its freedom, its temptation is to resort to new alliances with popular movements, or with parliamentary parties and pressure groups. This is the doubtful tendency today of 'Catholic Action' and of the 'Christian Democratic' parties in the new republics of Italy, France and Western Germany. It has been, over the past century or so, the doubtful tendency, too, of both the Established and Free Churches in England which, almost alone in Europe, have as yet been spared the worst experiences of adversity. But, even in this favoured corner of Christendom, the adversity of unemployment in the 'thirties shook to its foundations the old alliance between Methodism and the Labour movement, by seeming to disappoint their common hope for the kind of Ruskinian co-operative commonwealth which had been the ideal of so much English so-called socialism. And it would be strange if the worse disillusionments of Europe had not more powerfully discouraged the tendency to political alliances in the mind of continental Christians; perhaps we are witnessing today, throughout Europe, a revival of the primitive Christian sense of the incompatibility between all ideologies and the Christian hope, whether they be the dogmas of Leviathan or the vaguer ideals of 'liberal democracy'.

2

Here, then, ends our study of dualism and the Moral State. Of course, the historical method we have used for it proves nothing; it can be no more than a method of presentation. But the method has its uses at a time when men are conscious of facing an issue between two opposite principles of government, but are not very sure how to define it. English-speaking men and women today commonly think of themselves as belonging to a 'free world' and as committed to its defence against a rival world of communism. Communism they think they can define well enough, for it has its scriptures, its authoritative preachers of theory and its ruthless exponents of practice; but 'freedom' has been little more to them than a native climate, so variable as to elude definition. The "freedom from fear and want" of the Atlantic Charter is a definition in terms of ends rather than of means, and those terms, like Wilson's idea of a "world safe for democracy" can make little difference to the conduct of rulers who believe that means are justified by ends. And what planner of a Welfare State does not instinctively believe that?

At such a time, the Free World may well pause to re-value its assets and its responsibilities, in the light of history. Its citizens may usefully remember that, in the historic experience of their civilization, the issue has been one of means, rather than of ends: that the freedom of the individual in society has been regarded as the essential means, not only to a good life, but to the perfection of humanity; that the individual has been thus free only within the framework of a defined moral order, which he knows and accepts; that he has found this freedom in States dedicated to the maintenance of that order and has lost it in States which have claimed to be themselves the instruments of perfection; and that this claim has never been more dangerously made than in the last century and a half, when the individual has been incited to sink his conscience and his will in a monster of State sovereignty where he may forget his identity in the intoxication of corporate power.

Still more, the would-be Free World of today may usefully remember that, in the last two thousand years, the ideas of a good life and the perfection of humanity have acquired a new meaning and a new reality in human thought: that, in that thought, freedom has become the individual's way of access to God, and the moral order no more, but no less, than, as it were, the hedges that mark the outer limits of his way; that, within these limits, the freedom of the individual has been chiefly prized (to vary the metaphor) as the means to a re-creative change in man's very nature; and that this change has been conceived as accomplishing itself in a form of association which neither is the State, nor can be produced out of the State by any extension or refinement of its law.

This belief, since it first came to men's minds, has been at the heart of their love of liberty; it had been the intellectual foundation of all genuine philosophies of freedom. From it have emerged all those forms of dualism which are fused into the political life of the British commonwealth of nations: not only the dualism between Church and State, but the dualism between Crown and Parliament, between local and national self-government, between State services and voluntary co-operation. By contrast, without it, liberty has been little more than an opportunist catchword of many meanings; never a political principle which can command the intellectual assent of successive generations of citizens, or give a consistent direction to the policy of governments. Without it, liberty has been the party motto both of conservatives who are at ease in Zion and of radicals who envy them their ease; it has been the battle-cry both of oppressed nationalists, in revolt against alien rule, and of liberated nationalists, bent on the conquest of new territory; it has been the prudential maxim both of economists intent upon the optimum production of wealth in a competitive world and of industrial corporations equally intent on eliminating competition – but in none of these guises can it be an effective answer to the religious gospel of communism. Indeed, has it not been the characteristic slogan of all those 'bourgeois' revolutions which Marx recognized as the necessary forerunners of communism itself?

3

Revaluing thus its assets and responsibilities of belief, the Free World, in these days of pessimism, may do well to remember that, in the very age of Leviathan, its philosophy of freedom and law has spread from Western Europe to Asia and Africa; and that it is still powerful there beneath the surface of revolutionary change. The dangerous subordination of human personality to technological development and the crazy heresy of nationalism are not the only lessons which the West has taught to the ancient civilizations of the East or the nascent civilization of Africa. It has taught them this philosophy also, and the prime duty of its citizens is to show that they still believe what they have taught.

In our historical survey, we have not dealt with the external relations of Christendom. To have followed that tangled thread would have led us too far; but a word must be said about it here. For eleven hundred years, from the eighth to the nineteenth century, the civilization of Western Europe was bounded on the east and south by a curtain as real as the iron curtain of our day, the curtain which veiled the puritan totalism of Islam. That, after all, has been the essential character of Islam. It has often been tolerant; it has often given freedom of thought to scholars; it has almost always, to the delight of Englishmen, favoured the growth in private life of those simple integrities which make a 'gentleman'. But the States it has created have had no law but a religious law and, on the other hand, its religion has created no church but the State. This combination of an unalterable law with an omnipotent State has left no scope for the development of any sense of political commonwealth, or any standard of political morality. It teaches the brotherhood of man, but it has found political expression only in fighting empires and principalities. It has needed no Western tutors to teach it the essential characteristics of totalist nationalism.

It is difficult for this generation to realize how thick the curtain of Islam still was, even at the beginning of the twentieth century. It had recently been drawn back from all Africa except Tripoli and Cyrenaica, but it still stretched from the Adriatic to the Red Sea. Since the sixteenth century, however, it had begun to be outflanked along the coasts of Africa and India, and beyond. There, in the nineteenth century, the West, penetrating inland from the sea-boards, set itself to impress its characteristic pattern of dualism – in Asia, on mixed populations whose only experience of settled government in modern times had been that of Muslim rulers – in Africa, on 'primitive' tribes whose only contact with civilization had been with Muslim merchants and slave-raiders. Such an impression could be made only by direct demonstration, by the actual exercise of the authority of government. That was the effect, though not always the deliberate purpose, of what it is now fashionable to call 'imperialism' or 'colonialism'; and that has been, in spite of its blunders and crimes, its sufficient justification in the eyes of history.

It could, by its very nature, be only a passing phase, as the earlier British administrators in India foresaw. But it was, generally speaking, a necessary phase. Where, as in China and Japan, contact between East and West remained purely commercial and cultural, or even religious, the impression was not made. It was made in the Sudan, but not in Egypt. When the curtain was finally torn down in 1912–18 it was too late to make it in Syria and Mesopotamia; and the 'fertile crescent' from the Nile to the Persian Gulf was left to the barren nationalism of the Arab

League, intensified by the intrusion of an ambiguous Zionism. That the Western pattern has, nevertheless, in some sort, emerged in Turkey, proves only that no historical generalization can be wholly true.

Today these imprints of Western government in Asia and Africa are evidently in danger of being washed away by the tide of communist propaganda and conspiracy; but they are in even greater danger of being defaced by the muddle-headedness or the intellectual treachery of their authors themselves. Too many of their English-speaking authors, in particular, have forgotten what they once believed, and have turned to chatter about 'democracy'.

The clearest example of this danger is, perhaps, in southern and central Africa: the Africa of the 'colour bar'. Recently an African from Johannesburg has written despairingly, using language learnt from long residence in England:

The Blacks of the plural societies are determined to be free. And time and history are on their side. Is democracy against them?[1]

But of course it is. Colour prejudice, in itself, is as real as class prejudice, but hardly more intractable. In a free society, where differentiation is natural and where scope is given to the powerful solvent of Christian charity, it yields slowly, but it yields. Those who do not think in absolutes have seen it yield, over the last half-century, in the United States, in Jamaica, in West Africa, in Southern Rhodesia, even in Kenya. In such a society, the only mistake to be avoided is the nineteenth-century delusion, embodied in a once famous Kipling verse, that the development of 'backward' peoples must necessarily be slow. Sometimes, as we are now seeing, the pace of their development may quicken dizzily. But democracy is not a free society. It disdains Christian charity and knows no unity but that of assimilation. *Apartheid* is not, at root, a colour policy; it is the policy of a total nationalism

---

[1] Peter Abrahams. *Return to Goli*, Faber 1953.

and the colour bar is far from being the most sinister of its manifestations. That, as so often before in the last one hundred and fifty years, is the real issue. The sting of the colour bar is nationalism, and the strength of nationalism is democracy. Yet too much of 'left' political opinion in England seems bent today on inoculating Africans themselves with the same virus of totalism. The result may well be that the lead in enlightened colonial administration in Africa will pass from British hands into those of a younger parliamentary State and an older missionary church: the constitutional monarchy of Catholic Belgium.

4

Scope for Christian charity is, perhaps, the best description of the impulse which has given to the English section, at least, of the Free World another of its characteristic assets: the asset which, now that we are in danger of losing it, we have learnt to call the Welfare State.

In this matter, English thought has been fairly consistent. Wealth is best distributed, as well as produced, by free enterprise. Residual poverty, ignorance and distress are best relieved by the voluntary co-operation of groups or the benevolence of individuals. Nevertheless, poverty, ignorance and distress are dangers to the State; and, if they outgrow the resources of private benevolence, they must be remedied by State action. But the State must deal with them, so far as possible, in the spirit and by the methods of private benevolence and voluntary co-operation: in the spirit of a man's personal responsibility for his neighbour, and by the method of free response to each individual's needs. Hence the outstanding examples of British social policy in the past: its national system of poor relief, entrusted to the discretion of local neighbours; its system of voluntary hospitals and 'friendly' societies; and its national service of school teaching, whose members are not civil servants and are, in principle, free to deal with the children committed to their care as their professional skill and their sense of personal responsibility may suggest.

We are finding it so difficult to preserve this asset today that we are in danger of forgetting its existence. We came near to dissipating it in the mid-nineteenth century at its very source, by devising a fictitious form of legal association for the production and distribution of wealth: the limited liability company, whose shareholders have neither the duty nor the right to concern themselves either with the processes of production or with the salaries and wages of the producers. In law, the shareholders who constitute such a company are neither partners nor proprietors; they are simple creditors, with an equitable interest only in the profits of production. Current profit (as opposed even to the prudent administration of property) is therefore the only interest which the law recognizes in the shareholder. This is the real sting of contemporary attacks on the 'profit motive'; it is an attack upon a bad law which denies to the investor of capital any part in the vital human relationship of employer and employed. For the responsibilities of that relationship the State has been forced to substitute its own regulations enforcing minimum conditions of employment, together with a system of legalized warfare for the settlement of wages and hours of labour.

From that nineteenth-century mistake has flowed all our twentieth-century pre-occupation with State planning. In our crowd civilization, State planning seems hardly more impersonal than the policies of industrial associations, local authorities or co-operative groups, and tends to be substituted for them without counting any cost but that of public finance. But there is another cost: the cost of substituting a Physical Welfare State for the Moral State.

The fundamental aim of the State is moral improvement. It follows that the primary task of its law is to regulate relations between individuals, for it is between individuals that moral duties are performed or neglected. The claim of the State on the individual is not, in that sense, a moral claim; it is a claim to obedience. That word has been so over-issued for centuries that it has almost lost currency in our days. It does not properly describe the obligation undertaken in a contract of service, or the respect or deference due from one individual to another in many human relationships. Man owes obedience only to God and to such human authority as has, in the words of a Puritan governor of Massachusetts, "a stamp upon it from God". The State is, perhaps, not the only authority that can make this claim, but it is the only one that can, and must, make it over all men within its jurisdiction, irrespective of their own choice.

That claim, being absolute in its nature, would be intolerable if it were not limited in its scope. It is a dangerous half-truth that freedom depends, not on the volume of the State's commands, but on their quality. Under the best laws, much-governed men are less free than lightly governed men, for, whenever the law converts (as it often must) an obligation to a fellow-citizen into an obligation to the State, it substitutes a claim to obedience for the give-and-take of mutual rights and duties between individuals. That fact is faithfully reflected in one much criticized feature of English law: the denial of the citizen's right to sue the State. Whatever relaxations of that rule may be desirable, the rule itself is a salutary reminder that there can, in the nature of things, be no true mutuality in the relations of a citizen to his government – that, indeed, his relation to his government is best described by the discredited word 'subject'.

This is one of the corrupting tendencies of State Planning: its tendency to dissolve a personal sense of duty into a compulsory 'sentiment of sociability' – a 'social conscience' which is directed by the State and is limited to what the State can effectively undertake, and has, consequently, no immediate relation to personal conduct. Another tendency follows from it. In so far as this social conscience moves the individual citizen at all, it moves him, not to make sacrifices, but to demand them from others. The statesman, remembering his moral function, must judge the probable moral effect upon his citizens, not only of law itself, but also of the processes by which law is made and enforced. Both in the making and the enforcement of law, he must beware lest, in seeking to give outlets to the Christian spirit of a Christian nation, he deforms it by the very opportunities he offers it.

In the making of law, he must count it a tragedy that so many programmes of social righteousness become, under the conditions of parliamentary government, mere appeals to the crude self-interest of majorities at the expense of minorities. It must seem to him an even worse tragedy that, as the Welfare State multiplies its 'crimes' and creates more and more specialized services to correct them, the makers of the law become less and less conscious of the cost in individual suffering that has to be paid for its enforcement. They dismiss as almost silly any objection to the use of compulsion on individuals or groups where any social end is to be gained. Indeed, the social conscience illustrates the real nature of the 'altruism' which Comte alleged to be natural to man. It is an altruism of purpose, but not of means. In its pursuit of equality and the greatest good of the greatest number, it treats every free form of human life and association, not *prima facie* as something to be loved and fostered, but *prima facie* as a 'privilege' to be suppressed. It is quite ruthless in its dealings with the anomalous individual and, still more, with the anomalous group; and, of all groups, the family is in constant danger of being regarded as the most anomalous. For, as our bitter experience in the administration of 'means tests' should have taught us, in their family needs and (so to speak) their family policies, men neither are nor desire to be equal. There can, after all, be no deeper contrast than between the temper of Christian brotherhood and this civic altruism which so complacently normalizes compulsion.

Of such are the real problems of the Planned Welfare State. If we recognize them for what they are, we shall mobilize our assets to solve them, and our assets are still sufficient to ensure success. We shall, for instance, succeed in mobilizing a Health Service which will bring within the reach of all citizens, not only the best scientific treatment in hospitals, but effective human advice in their homes. On the other hand, if we liquidate our assets in a blind attempt to magnify the responsibility and authority of the State, we shall establish a tyranny less absolute, perhaps, but even less moral than that of totalist communism. The conclusion of all that has been written in this essay is that the difference between good and bad government lies, not in what men from time to time devise, but in what they believe. If what they believe embraces political philosophy, but transcends it, their least satisfactory devices to meet the needs of the moment will do little permanent harm; on the other hand, their best devices will turn to their ruin if, for lack of any deeper belief, they inflate them into principles. The Free World today is more imminently threatened by a corruption of belief at its own heart than by any communist attack from without.

Q

CHAPTER 18

The choice

The fundamental issue of belief: the re-creation of human nature.

There is one final word to be said. Among all the Free World's political assets of belief and responsibility, the greatest is the belief which is beyond politics: the belief in the re-creation of human nature. Is it an intolerable paradox that good statesmanship should thus depend absolutely on belief in a scheme of human destiny, to be accomplished, indeed, in this world, but towards the accomplishment of which statesmanship can make only a subordinate contribution? Subordinate; but essential. It is surely no small thing that the Christian governor and the Christian citizen should be thus enabled to see their due place in the whole purpose of God. It is no small thing that their work should be dignified by the assurance that they are, indeed, God's ministers, and that the Moral State is, indeed, a revelation of the righteousness of God. And it is no small thing that the citizen should be thus given the right to claim that he has higher duties than the law can enforce, for the performance of which the law must leave him free. Anyway, this is the inescapable dualism to which the Free World is committed. From the dilemma between this dualism and the totalist democracy of the Unfree World there is, in truth, no escape, save an escape from hope itself.

Of course, to argue that men have to choose between two alternatives of belief is not to pretend to prove that either alternative is true. Such a pretension would be suicidal; the responsibilities of belief cannot be founded on an irresponsible pragmatism. After all, it is perfectly possible to live, and to live nobly, by a philosophy which discards hope. The classic example of such a philosophy is the Stoic acceptance (in the words of Marcus Aurelius) of the "monotonous and meaningless rhythm of the universe". But a better example is, perhaps, the Book of Ecclesiastes. Man's aspirations (so runs its argument) are vanity: he cannot make the crooked straight, nor save himself or his neighbour from perishing like the beasts. There is a God, but one too remote for his knowledge, almost too remote even for his prayer. Yet God has given him two modest gifts: a craftsman's skill and a simple moral law. Let him rejoice in the one and obey the other, for that is his whole duty. Such Stoicism may be a 'spiritual vacuum',[1] but the historian cannot demonstrate that it is untrue.

All he can do is to suggest that different beliefs tend to result in, or at least to be associated with, different forms of political action, or lack of action. By that test, he must classify Stoicism as a philosophy of the twilight, of the last days of dying systems when men are weary of action and do not care to look ahead. And such last days are not commonly days of good government. Stoicism is the empty house of the parable, open to strange hauntings of aimless cruelty and heartless benevolence. It is not really an alternative social philosophy, but merely a denial that such a philosophy is possible.

And the same is true of many more positive social beliefs, like the various pre-Marxist theories of progress and human perfectibility, or the quite modern theory of the 'new evolution'. Such theories do not discard hope, but they generally pitch hope low – low enough to be arguably within the reach of 'natural' human character. Aiming thus no higher than, as it were, the reasonable domestication of a once wild animal, they tone down the contradiction in man's nature, his contrasted capacities for good and evil, to the mild water-colours of a civilized scepticism, until the historian can no longer recognize in their polite picture

---

[1] Arnold Toynbee. *The World and the West*. O.U.P. 1952.

any likeness to the actual record of human government. He must classify the devotees of these theories, too, as philosophers of the twilight, though with a difference. No less than Stoics, they herald catastrophe; only, unlike the Stoic pessimist, they are unconscious heralds, whom catastrophe takes always by surprise.

On the whole, then, the historian must incline to the view that, at any given moment, political man is, in truth, confined to a choice between only two alternatives of belief. Of course, the alternatives present themselves in rather different forms to different societies and at different epochs; but the movement of civilization seems to be towards a narrowing and sharpening of the choice. This is the quality of the choice, today, between the Free World and the Unfree. In this study the choice has been presented in Christian terms, both because the civilization which is at the heart of the Free World is still a Christian civilization and because it is in Christian terms that the issue presents itself at its sharpest. It does not present itself in quite the same terms to all the member societies of the Free World. India, for instance, has taken the imprint of Western dualism, not because it has, on the whole, been presented to her people in Christian terms, but because their native religions have taught them from time immemorial to think of the duty and destiny of man, at least individually, in terms of sin and law and deliverance. How the issue will sharpen itself in such a society we cannot foresee. But in Christian societies the issue has always been clear and sharp enough; only, today, perhaps, it is presented to them for the last time and for their final choice.

And the choice is in doubt. Even for those who hold the Christian hope, it is not to Christian *civilization* that security has been promised against the gates of hell. The choice today seems to hang uncertainly on two opposite tendencies. We have seen that, throughout the history of Christendom, the distinctive Christian hope of perfection, within which government and law assume their due proportions, however potent it has been within the 'holy communion' of believers, has been peculiarly liable to corruption in its contacts with the world of politics. Its character-istic corruption has been the ideology of what we have called the Augustinian Church. In our own times, that ideology has tended to be revived in a 'democratic' form. The idea of re-creation has been dismissed as being 'beyond history' and therefore irrelevant to the practical problems of society, while the Kingdom of God has been equated with the best versions that reforming politicians can offer of "mean things and mortal and things as they are". Yet, on the other hand, we are now, perhaps, beginning to discover, as Christians have repeatedly discovered in earlier ages of the Church's history, that this habit of mind takes all the savour out of Christian life. It leaves Christians in much the same frame of mind as the Jewry of two thousand years ago. As that people looked for a Messianic deliverer who would preserve and glorify an existing Jewish cultural and commercial empire, with its dis-tinctive law and its elaborate ecclesiastical institutions, stretching through Asia Minor and North Africa into Europe and linking Parthia with Rome – so we have looked for a 'purpose of God in history' which will vindicate a Christian civilization, with its anointed kings or educated democracies, its mitred bishops and its missionary churches, its potential economic plenty, its trade union organization and its schemes of fundamental social reform. But we are now realizing that there seems to be as little place for the Risen Christ in this second picture as there was for the Incar-nate Christ in the first.

Under the shock of that realization, the Christian Church may be once more experiencing a Change of Mind, not widely different from the change it provoked at its first appearance in the world of the Roman Empire. As then, the change will not be provoked by prudential considerations of 'moral re-armament' or the like, nor will it be recognizable as a renaissance of Western civilization in response to a communist challenge. As then, it may well be, on the face of it, politically useless, or even inconvenient. Yet, as then it may restore the savour of liberty to a would-be Free World where the pervasive influence of centralizing States threatens to extinguish the 'private and local wisdoms' which were once their strength; and it may offer even to an Unfree World the attractions of a 'holy communion' at once more stable and more vivid than the uneasy self-assertions of democratic citizenship. For those today who wistfully assume that not even the Free World is any longer a Christian world misread their history. It is no longer an Augustinian world; but it may, for that very reason, be the more sensitive to the meaning of Sir Thomas Browne's quaint injunction: "Swell not out into actions which embroil and confound the earth, but be of those violent ones that force the kingdom of heaven."

Date Due

MR 15 7			

Demco 293-5